In this volume, Lave and Wenger undertake a radical and important rethinking and reformulation of our conception of learning. By placing emphasis on the whole person, and by viewing agent, activity, and world as mutually constitutive, they give us the opportunity to escape from the tyranny of the assumption that learning is the reception of factual knowledge or information. The authors argue that most accounts of learning have ignored its quintessentially social character. To make the crucial step away from a solely epistemological account of the person, they propose that learning is a process of participation in communities of practice, participation that is at first legitimately peripheral but that increases gradually in engagement and complexity.

Situated Learning

Learning in Doing: Social, Cognitive, and Computational Perspectives

Senior Editor Emeritus
JOHN SEELY BROWN, *Xerox Palo Alto Research Center*

General Editors
ROY PEA, *Professor of Education and the Learning Sciences and Director, Stanford Center for Innovations in Learning, Stanford University*
CHRISTIAN HEATH, *The Management Centre, King's College, London*
LUCY A. SUCHMAN, *Centre for Science Studies and Department of Sociology, Lancaster University, UK*

Continued on page following the Index

Situated Learning
Legitimate Peripheral Participation

JEAN LAVE
ETIENNE WENGER

CAMBRIDGE
UNIVERSITY PRESS

CAMBRIDGE UNIVERSITY PRESS
Cambridge, New York, Melbourne, Madrid, Cape Town,
Singapore, São Paulo, Delhi, Tokyo, Mexico City

Cambridge University Press
32 Avenue of the Americas, New York, NY 10013-2473, USA

www.cambridge.org
Information on this title: www.cambridge.org/9780521423748

First published 1991
24th printing 2011

Printed in the United States of America

A catalog record for this publication is available from the British Library.

ISBN 978-0-521-41308-4 Hardback
ISBN 978-0-521-42374-8 Paperback

It occurred to us at the same moment to dedicate this book to each other. We do so as a celebration of an extraordinarily happy collaboration, in which we experienced many of the things we were writing about.

Contents

9

Contents

Series Foreword

The *situated* nature of learning, remembering, and understanding is a central fact. It may appear obvious that human minds develop in social situations, and that they use the tools and representational media that culture provides to support, extend, and reorganize mental functioning. But cognitive theories of knowledge representation and educational practice, in school and in the workplace, have not been sufficiently responsive to questions about these relationships. And the need for responsiveness has become salient as computational media radically reshape the frontiers of individual and social action, and as educational achievement fails to translate into effective use of knowledge.

This series is born of the conviction that new and exciting interdisciplinary syntheses are under way, as scholars and practitioners from diverse fields seek to analyze and influence the new transformations of social and mental life, and to understand successful learning wherever it occurs.

Computational media include not only computers but the vast array of expressive, receptive, and presentational devices available for use with computers, including interactive video, optical media such as CD-ROM and CD-I, networks, hypermedia systems, work-group collaboration tools, speech recognition and synthesis, image processing and animation, and software more generally.

These technologies are dramatically transforming the basic patterns of communication and knowledge interchange in societies, and automating the component processes of thinking and problem solving. In changing situations of knowledge acquisition and use, the new interactive technologies redefine – in ways yet to be determined – what it means to know and understand, and what it means to become "literate" or an "educated citizen."

The series invites contributions that advance our understanding of these seminal issues.

Roy Pea
John Seely Brown

Foreword by William F. Hanks

I first encountered these ideas in spring of 1990, when Jean
Lave spoke at the Workshop on Linguistic Practice at the University of Chicago. There were about a dozen of us, mostly
working on problems in language use and interaction; mostly
anthropologists, linguists, or hybrids; several with research
commitments to a non-Western language. I had just completed
a study of reference as a social practice, in which I analyzed
Yucatec Maya language use in its linguistic, indexical, and
cultural contexts (1990). One of the central issues being pur-
sued in the workshop was the relation between context and
literal meaning or, in somewhat more technical terms, the role
of indexicality in semantics. Coming from this angle, Lave
and Wenger's work was really exciting because it located
learning squarely in the processes of coparticipation, not in the
heads of individuals. The analogy to language was just below
the surface, only occasionally made explicit during several hours
of very fruitful discussion, and yet many of us felt that we had
gained new insights into problems of language. We had already been exploring speech as interaction, trying to take
meaning production out of the heads of individual speakers
and locate it in the fields of social interaction. The 1990 pre-
sentation, and Jean Lave's ability to engage intellectually in

the issues it raised, provoked some of the best discussion we have enjoyed. My first reason for mentioning this background, then, is to say that this book, on which the speech was based, is very productive in the sense of setting forth a strong, provocative position on issues that are of basic significance to practice theory quite generally, and not only to how practice grounds learning. The second reason is simply to underscore the fact that my remarks in this foreword come from a certain perspective, and are necessarily selective.

Situated Learning contributes to a growing body of research in human sciences that explores the situated character of human understanding and communication. It takes as its focus the relationship between learning and the social situations in which it occurs. Rather than defining it as the acquisition of propositional knowledge, Lave and Wenger situate learning in certain forms of social coparticipation. Rather than asking what kinds of cognitive processes and conceptual structures are involved, they ask what kinds of social engagements provide the proper context for learning to take place. This shift has interesting consequences, which relate the book to a broad set of interdisciplinary issues.

On the one hand, it implies a highly interactive and productive role for the skills that are acquired through the learning process. The individual learner is not gaining a discrete body of abstract knowledge which (s)he will then transport and reapply in later contexts. Instead, (s)he acquires the skill to perform by actually engaging in the process, under the attenuated conditions of *legitimate peripheral participation*. This central concept denotes the particular mode of engagement of a learner who participates in the actual practice of an expert, but only to a limited degree and with limited responsibility for the ultimate product as a whole. There is no necessary implication

14

that a learner acquires mental representations that remain fixed thereafter, nor that the "lesson" taught consists itself in a set of abstract representations. On the contrary, Lave and Wenger seem to challenge us to rethink what it means to learn, indeed to rethink what it means to understand. On this point their project joins a growing literature in cognitive studies, discourse analysis, and sociolinguistics, which treats verbal meaning as the product of speakers' interpretive activities, and not merely as the "content" of linguistic forms. The common element here is the premise that meaning, understanding, and learning are all defined relative to actional contexts, not to self-contained structures.

On the other hand, the shift also alters the locus of learning. In a classical intellectualist theory, it is the individual mind that acquires mastery over processes of reasoning and description, by internalizing and manipulating structures. Like thinking, learning so construed takes place in the individual. Two people may well learn the same thing, just as they may derive what is for all practical purposes the same understanding, yet this is a matter of coincidence, not collaborative production. The challenge of this book is surely deeper: Learning is a process that takes place in a participation framework, not in an individual mind. This means, among other things, that it is mediated by the differences of perspective among the coparticipants. It is the community, or at least those participating in the learning context, who "learn" under this definition. Learning is, as it were, distributed among coparticipants, not a one-person act. While the apprentice may be the one transformed most dramatically by increased particpation in a productive process, it is the wider process that is the crucial locus and precondition for this transformation. How do the masters of apprentices themselves change through acting as colearners and, therefore, how does the skill being mastered change in the process? The larger community of practitioners reproduces itself through the formation of apprentices, yet it would presumably be transformed as well. Legitimate peripheral participation does not explain these changes, but it has the virtue of making them all but inevitable. Even in cases where a fixed doctrine is transmitted, the ability of a community to reproduce itself through the training process derives not from the doctrine, but from the maintenance of certain modes of coparticipation in which it is embedded.

As a corollary of these shifts, the framework of this book implies a constitutive role in learning for improvisation, actual cases of interaction, and emergent processes which cannot be reduced to generalized structures. Here it joins developments in those social sciences where phenomenological, interactive, and ''practice''-centered approaches have gained importance. One of the basic moves of such approaches has been to question the validity of descriptions of social behavior based on the enactment of prefabricated codes and structures. Instead, the focus on actors' productive contributions to social order has led naturally to a greater role for negotiation, strategy, and unpredictable aspects of action. This shift has far-reaching and as yet little-understood consequences for how one describes human thought, communication, and learning. The challenge, it would seem, is to rethink action in such a way that structure and process, mental representation and skillful execution, interpenetrate one another profoundly. It is important to see that Lave and Wenger reject both of the obvious extremes in responding to this challenge.

In a classical structural analysis, aspects of behavior are explained by, and serve as empirical evidence for, preexisting, ''underlying'' systems. It is these systems that provide the ob-

ject of which an analysis is a model. To the extent that actual
processes are analyzed, they are "structuralized" – made to
follow from, or instantiate, structures. The activity of understanding, in such a view, comes down to recognizing and implementing instances of structure, filling them in with an overlay
of situational particulars, and relating them to a "context"
(which is in turn structured). Insofar as "understanding" is
something a person does in his or her head, it ultimately involves the mental representations of individuals. Understanding is seen to arise out of the mental operations of a subject on
objective structures. Lave and Wenger reject this view of understanding insofar as they locate learning not in the acquisition of structure, but in the increased access of learners to participating roles in expert performances.

The other extreme position would be sheerly interactive,
rejecting altogether the premise that structures may preform
aspects of experience. Here, too, the position implicit in this
book is nuanced. For Lave and Wenger do not reject the notion
that participation frameworks are structured – it is precisely
this that provides the conditions for legitimate peripheral participation – nor do they deny that expert performance is systematic. The hard question is *what kind of system, and what
kind of structure?* It is not merely that the structural issue is
transposed from the level of mental representations to that of
participation frames. Rather, this transposition is compounded
by a more subtle and potentially radical shift from *invariant*
structures to ones that are less rigid and more deeply adaptive.
One way of phrasing this is to say that structure is more the
variable outcome of action than its invariant precondition.
Preexisting structures may vaguely determine thought, learning, or action, but only in an underspecified, highly schematic
way. And the structures may be significantly reconfigured in

the local context of action. Such a conception retains a constitutive role for the actual activities in which learners engage, while still avoiding the extreme position which denies any prefabricated content in what they learn.

Given this framework, learning could be viewed as a special *type* of social practice associated with the kind of participation frame designated legitimate peripheral participation (LPP). Under this reading, Lave and Wenger's proposal gives learning an actional ground, but retains its discreteness as a category of action. Alternatively, and clearly more in line with their goals, it can be viewed as a *feature* of practice, which might be present in all sorts of activities, not just in clear cases of training and apprenticeship. Think of all the everyday situations in which people coparticipate to a limited extent, thereby gaining access to modes of behavior not otherwise available to them, eventually developing skill adequate to certain kinds of performance. Participating members of religious congregations, athletes training together, the third string on a team, spectators at any public event, faculty and students in a university setting, new friends, the home *bricoleur* who helps a tradesperson repair his porch, nonmechanics when they describe the problems with their cars to mechanics, patients being treated by doctors − all of these interactions initially involve limited, highly asymmetric forms of coparticipation. All seem to have the potential to transform the participants, even if their trajectories and thresholds of change differ widely. In actual empirical studies of LPP, it will be important to consider critically the range of contexts it is meant to describe, from institutionally circumscribed training all the way to the learning immanent in everyday activities. At the latter extreme, both limited peripheral engagements and the potential for change would seem to be present whenever one party to an activity is more skilled more skilled or expert (in some relevant way) than another. Such a liberal reading of the LPP concept runs the risk of erasing its specificity, but has the advantage of tying it into all kinds of practice. Furthermore, one could suggest that learning would be likely to take place whenever people interact under conditions of LPP. This would imply that certain participation frameworks may be "dispositionally adapted" to producing learning, even if the coparticipants are not attempting to acquire or inculcate identifiable skills. Language acquisition, where the learner is a legitimate peripheral participant interacting with masterful speakers, may well involve this. A child interacting with adults and an outsider habituating himself to local ways of speaking may be submitting to and ultimately reproducing community standards of which they never become aware. This kind of pervasive, low-level learning can be seen when speakers acquire regional accents or turns of phrase despite themselves, or when students come to reproduce aspects of the performance style of a charismatic teacher. Clearly, on such a general reading of learning, the trajectories followed by those who learn will be extremely diverse and may not be predictable. The challenge for a community that seeks to reproduce itself would be to regiment the interactions in which learning is likely to occur, as well as the outcomes to which it may lead.

It is clear that in many learning contexts, even quite narrowly defined, participants may disengage before attaining mastery over core skills. In such cases, they may leave the learning context with some but not all of the relevant skills, transporting what they have learned into another context. The question seems to be how one describes the detachability of these skills from the participatory contexts in which they were acquired. If both learning and the subject learned are embedded in participation frameworks, then the portability of learned skills must rely on the commensurability of certain forms of participation. The employee who rises up through the ranks, performing a variety of tasks which she must later integrate as a manager, has in effect learned modes of acting and problem solving, not a system of rules or representations. Presumably, the success of a learner changing work contexts, and therefore integrating into new participation frameworks, would depend upon his or her ability to move between modes of coparticipation. This ability could be described in two quite different ways. One could assume that participation is schematized and that what is transported by the effective learner is an expanding repertoire of participation schemata. This reintroduces the notion of learning as structure acquisition. Alternatively, one could insist that participation is not schematized that way, and that what the effective learner learns is how to actually *do* practices. A schema cannot explain its own use, manipulation, or role in future improvisations. On this aspect, it seems necessary to posit that the skillful learner acquires something more like the ability to play various roles in various fields of participation. This would involve things other than schemata: ability to anticipate, a sense of what can feasibly occur within specified contexts, even if in a given case it does not occur. It involves a prereflective grasp of complex situations, which might be reported as a propositional description, but is not one itself. Mastery involves timing of actions relative to changing circumstances: the ability to improvise. By tying learning into participation, the notion of LPP leads us to think again about what it means for knowledge to be portable. Notice that the ability to engage in LPP, and the ability to learn, would presumably be acquired as well. The relative transparency of a learning context would depend not on features of the context per se, but on the preparedness and flexibility of the learner. (This is not to deny that contexts may be relatively transparent or opaque in terms of the level of preparedness they require on the part of a learner.)

Taken in relation to a single craft that is taught through "hands-on" legitimate peripheral participation, the ability to learn would develop in close relation to the ability to perform tasks. On the other hand, a training program that consists of instructional settings separated from actual performance would tend to split the learner's ability to manage the learning situation apart from his ability to perform the skill. Given a sufficient disjunction between the skill being taught and the actual performance situation, one could imagine an actor who becomes expert as a learner – that is, who becomes a master at managing the learning situation – but who never actually learns the performance skills themselves. This possibility seems to be what periodic tests of performance are supposed to guard against. In an apprenticeship relation, where the learner is actually performing routinely, this kind of abstract exam is less relevant.

Insofar as learning really does consist in the development of portable interactive skills, it can take place even when coparticipants fail to share a common code. The apprentice's ability to understand the master's performance depends not on their possessing the same representation of it, or of the objects it entails, but rather on their engaging in the performance in congruent ways. Similarly, the master's effectiveness at producing learning is not dependent on her ability to inculcate the student with her own conceptual representations. Rather, it depends on her ability to manage effectively a division of participation that provides for growth on the part of the student. Again, it would be this common ability to coparticipate that would provide the matrix for learning, not the commonality of symbolic or referential structures. (Of course the two may be interwoven in given cases, depending upon the nature of the skill.)

This last point raises a question about language in learning. In Chapter 4, Lave and Wenger rightly question the idea that verbal explanation is a uniquely effective mode of instruction, somehow superior to direct demonstration. Given the rest of their approach, the inverse claim would appear more natural. Quite simply, if learning is about increased access to performance, then the way to maximize learning is to perform, not to talk about it. The notion that demonstration is context specific and explanation context independent is based on an impoverished notion of both. A word of caution is merited here, lest Lave and Wenger's position be misunderstood, for this critique might appear to treat language as a code for *talking about* the world. As they recognize, a significant body of theory and research has shown that speech is equally a means of *acting in* the world. The point is germane, since language use entails multiple participatory skills, and is one of the most basic modes of access to interaction in social life. To equate discourse with reflections on action, instead of action itself, would be to fall prey to the very structural views that Lave and Wenger undermine in their approach to learning. Indeed, as they point out, the role of language in learning is likely to be highly differentiated, and a powerful source of evidence for the other ongoing modes of participation. At the least, the co-participants in communication among masters, learners, patients (etc.) provide part of the necessary background against which LPP must be defined. Once we see discourse production as a social and cultural practice, and not as a second-order representation of practice, it becomes clear that it must be configured along with other kinds of work in the overall matrix of performance. It also becomes important to investigate retellings and discussions that take place between and around performance events, and between learners and their respective communities. Rather than slipping back into the structure-acquisition model, such an investigation of language would contribute to a more deeply historicized account of situated learning.

Attention to linguistic action may also help sort out a very tricky question regarding LPP, namely, whether it designates a kind of role configuration that actors may engage in or, rather, a way of engaging. Students of conversation have shown that a single party to an interaction may simultaneously fill several roles, and that, under proper circumstances, a single role can be occupied by more than one interactant. To the extent that LPP works at the level of how roles are occupied, we would be inclined to say that it is a way of engaging, not a structure in which engagement takes place. As such, it may be characterized by the partiality of the apprentice's contribution to the whole, or by the fact that the apprentice is simultaneously attending to the task at hand and to how the master performs in relation to it. In other words, LPP is not a simple participation structure in which an apprentice occupies a particular role at the edge of a larger process. It is rather an interactive process in which the apprentice engages by simultaneously performing in *several roles* – status subordinate, learning practitioner, sole responsible agent in minor parts of the performance, aspiring expert, and so forth – each implying a different sort of responsibility, a different set of role relations, and a different interactive involvement. One would expect that the role configurations in which LPP takes place would differ widely through time and space, and even over the course of a single apprenticeship, yet the interactive *prise de conscience,* the way the learner places himself in relation to the whole, would remain consistent. Under such a view, LPP is not a structure, no matter how subtly defined, but rather a way of acting in the world which takes place under widely varying conditions.

This last remark raises a final, still broader suggestion that is implicit in the book, namely, that learning is a way of being in the social world, not a way of coming to know about it. Learners, like observers more generally, are engaged both in the contexts of their learning and in the broader social world within which these contexts are produced. Without this engagement, there is no learning, and where the proper engagement is sustained, learning will occur. Just as making theory is a form of practice in the world, not a speculation at a remove from it, so too learning is a practice, or a family of them. This entailment of Lave and Wenger's provocative book brings it into line with important developments in a range of other human sciences.

William F. Hanks
University of Chicago

Acknowledgments

The idea of exploring and developing the notion of legitimate peripheral participation would not have happened in any other context but that in which we were both working in 1988: the Institute for Research on Learning in Palo Alto, California. In particular, an ongoing reading group on activity theory, critical psychology, and learning in the workplace was a wonderful source of ideas and discussion. We wish to thank Yrjo Engeström, Chandra Mukerji, and Michael Cole, the organizers of a conference on Work and Communication at the University of California, San Diego, in July 1988, where we presented the first formulation of our ideas. We are grateful, both to organizers and participants, for the opportunity to discuss these ideas with them, and especially to Aaron Cicourel for his helpful suggestions for revising our first draft. We also wish to thank Stephen Shapin and Adi Ophir, the conveners of a Workshop on the Place of Knowledge, at the Van Leer Institute in Jerusalem in May of 1989, which provided us with an opportunity to push our thinking further. Above all, we wish to thank the readers of our successive drafts, too numerous to address individually, for their discussions and comments and for their willingness to share our enthusiasm while providing

25

Acknowledgments

constructive critiques. Two names must be mentioned, however. We give special thanks to Ole Dreier, who greatly helped us deepen our thinking by writing us a ''paper'' about our paper, and to Paul Duguid, that rare colleague whose editorial involvement became akin to coauthorship.

Jean Lave
Etienne Wenger

1

Legitimate Peripheral Participation

Legitimate Peripheral Participation

Learning viewed as situated activity has as its central defining characteristic a process that we call *legitimate peripheral participation*. By this we mean to draw attention to the point that learners inevitably participate in communities of practitioners and that the mastery of knowledge and skill requires newcomers to move toward full participation in the sociocultural practices of a community. "Legitimate peripheral participation" provides a way to speak about the relations between newcomers and old-timers, and about activities, identities, artifacts, and communities of knowledge and practice. It concerns the process by which newcomers become part of a community of practice. A person's intentions to learn are engaged and the meaning of learning is configured through the process of becoming a full participant in a sociocultural practice. This social process includes, indeed it subsumes, the learning of knowledgeable skills.

In order to explain our interest in the concept of legitimate peripheral participation, we will try to convey a sense of the perspectives that it opens and the kinds of questions that it raises. A good way to start is to outline the history of the concept as it has become increasingly central to our thinking about issues of learning. Our initial intention in writing what has gradually evolved into this book was to rescue the idea of *apprenticeship*. In 1988, notions about apprenticeship were flying around the halls of the Institute for Research on Learning, acting as a token of solidarity and as a focus for discussions on the nature of learning. We and our colleagues had begun to talk about learners as apprentices, about teachers and computers as masters, and about cognitive apprenticeship, apprenticeship learning, and even life as apprenticeship. It was evident that no one was certain what the term meant. Furthermore, it was understood to be a synonym for *situated learning,* about which we were equally uncertain. Resort to one did not clarify the other. Apprenticeship had become yet another panacea for a broad spectrum of learning-research problems, and it was in danger of becoming meaningless.

Other considerations motivated this work as well. Our own earlier work on craft apprenticeship in West Africa, on intelligent tutoring systems, and on the cultural transparency of technology seemed relevant and at the same time insufficient for the development of an adequate theory of learning, giving us an urgent sense that we needed such a theory. Indeed, our central ideas took shape as we came to see that the most interesting features both of apprenticeship and of "glass-box" approaches to the development and understanding of technology could be characterized – and analyzed – as legitimate peripheral participation in communities of practice.

The notion that learning through apprenticeship was a matter of legitimate peripheral participation arose first in research on craft apprenticeship among Vai and Gola tailors in Liberia (Lave, in preparation). In that context it was simply an observation about the tailors' apprentices within an analysis addressing questions of how apprentices might engage in a common, structured pattern of learning experiences without being taught, examined, or reduced to mechanical copiers of everyday tailoring tasks, and of how they become, with remarkably few exceptions, skilled and respected master tailors. It was difficult, however, to separate the historically and culturally specific circumstances that made Vai and Gola apprenticeship both effective and benign as a form of education from the critique of schooling and school practices that this inevitably suggested, or from a more general theory of situated learning.

This added to the general confusion that encouraged us to undertake this project.

Over the past two years we have attempted to clarify the confusion. Two moments in that process were especially important. To begin with, the uses of "apprenticeship" in cognitive and educational research were largely metaphorical, even though apprenticeship as an actual educational form clearly had a long and varied train of historically and culturally specific realizations. We gradually became convinced that we needed to reexamine the relationship between the "apprenticeship" of speculation and historical forms of apprenticeship. This led us to insist on the distinction between our theoretical framework for analyzing educational forms and specific historical instances of apprenticeship. This in turn led us to explore learning as "situated learning."

Second, this conception of situated learning clearly was more encompassing in intent than conventional notions of "learning *in situ*" or "learning by doing" for which it was used as a rough equivalent. But, to articulate this intuition usefully, we needed a better characterization of "situatedness" as a theoretical perspective. The attempt to clarify the concept of situated learning led to critical concerns about the theory and to further revisions that resulted in the move to our present view that learning is an integral and inseparable aspect of social practice. We have tried to capture this new view under the rubric of legitimate peripheral participation.

Discussing each shift in turn may help to clarify our reasons for coming to characterize learning as legitimate peripheral participation in communities of practice.

Situated Learning

Fashioning a firm distinction between historical *forms* of apprenticeship and situated learning as a historical–cultural *theory* required that we stop trying to use empirical cases of apprenticeship as a lens through which to view all forms of learning. On these grounds we started to reconsider the forms of apprenticeship with which we were most familiar as models of effective learning in the context of a broader theoretical goal. Nevertheless, specific cases of apprenticeship were of vital interest in the process of developing and exemplifying a theory of situated learning and we thus continued to use some of these studies as resources in working out our ideas. We might equally have turned to studies of socialization; children are, after all, quintessentially legitimate peripheral participants in adult social worlds. But various forms of apprenticeship seemed to capture very well our interest in learning in situated ways – in the transformative possibilities of being and becoming complex, full cultural–historical participants in the world – and it would be difficult to think of a more apt range of social practices for this purpose.

The distinction between historical cases of apprenticeship and a theory of situated learning was strengthened as we developed a more comprehensive view of different approaches to situatedness. Existing confusion over the meaning of situated learning and, more generally, situated activity resulted from differing interpretations of the concept. On some occasions "situated" seemed to mean merely that some of people's thoughts and actions were located in space and time. On other occasions, it seemed to mean that thought and action were social only in the narrow sense that they involved other people, or that they were immediately dependent for meaning on

32

the social setting that occasioned them. These types of interpretations, akin to naive views of indexicality, usually took some activities to be situated and some not.

In the concept of situated activity we were developing, however, the situatedness of activity appeared to be anything but a simple empirical attribute of everyday activity or a corrective to conventional pessimism about informal, experience-based learning. Instead, it took on the proportions of a general theoretical perspective, the basis of claims about the relational character of knowledge and learning, about the negotiated character of meaning, and about the concerned (engaged, dilemma-driven) nature of learning activity for the people involved. That perspective meant that there is no activity that is not situated. It implied emphasis on comprehensive understanding involving the whole person rather than "receiving" a body of factual knowledge about the world; on activity in and with the world; and on the view that agent, activity, and the world mutually constitute each other.

We have discovered that this last conception of situated activity and situated learning, which has gradually emerged in our understanding, frequently generates resistance, for it seems to carry with it connotations of parochialism, particularity, and the limitations of a given time and task. This misinterpretation of situated learning requires comment. (Our own objections to theorizing in terms of situated learning are somewhat different. These will become clearer shortly.) The first point to consider is that even so-called general knowledge only has power in specific circumstances. Generality is often associated with abstract representations, with decontextualization. But abstract representations are meaningless unless they can be made specific to the situation at hand. Moreover, the formation or acquisition of an abstract principle is itself a specific event in specific circumstances. Knowing a general rule by itself in no way assures that any generality it may carry is enabled in the specific circumstances in which it is relevant. In this sense, any "power of abstraction" is thoroughly situated, in the lives of persons and in the culture that makes it possible. On the other hand, the world carries its own structure so that specificity always implies generality (and in this sense generality is not to be assimilated to abstractness): That is why stories can be so powerful in conveying ideas, often more so than an articulation of the idea itself. What is called general knowledge is not privileged with respect to other "kinds" of knowledge. It too can be gained only in specific circumstances. And it too must be brought into play in specific circumstances. The generality of any form of knowledge always lies in the power to renegotiate the meaning of the past and future in constructing the meaning of present circumstances.

FROM SITUATED LEARNING TO LEGITIMATE PERIPHERAL PARTICIPATION

This brings us to the second shift in perspective that led us to explore learning as legitimate peripheral participation. The notion of situated learning now appears to be a transitory concept, a bridge, between a view according to which cognitive processes (and thus learning) are primary and a view according to which social practice is the primary, generative phenomenon, and learning is one of its characteristics. There is a significant contrast between a theory of learning in which practice (in a narrow, replicative sense) is subsumed within processes of learning and one in which learning is taken to be an integral aspect of practice (in a historical, generative sense). In our view, learning is not merely situated in practice – as if it were some independently reifiable process that just happened to be located somewhere; learning is an integral part of generative social practice in the lived-in world. The problem – and the central preoccupation of this monograph – is to translate this into a specific analytic approach to learning. Legitimate peripheral participation is proposed as a descriptor of engagement in social practice that entails learning as an integral constituent.

Before proceeding with a discussion of the analytic questions involved in a social practice theory of learning, we need to discuss our choices of terms and the issues that they reflect, in order to clarify our conception of legitimate peripheral participation. Its composite character, and the fact that it is not difficult to propose a contrary for each of its components, may be misleading. It seems all too natural to decompose it into a set of three contrasting pairs: legitimate versus illegitimate, peripheral versus central, participation versus nonparticipation. But we intend for the concept to be taken as a whole. Each of its aspects is indispensable in defining the others and cannot be considered in isolation. Its constituents contribute inseparable aspects whose combinations create a landscape – shapes, degrees, textures – of community membership.

Thus, in the terms proposed here there may very well be no such thing as an "illegitimate peripheral participant." The form that the legitimacy of participation takes is a defining characteristic of ways of belonging, and is therefore not only a crucial condition for learning, but a constitutive element of its content. Similarly, with regard to "peripherality" there may well be no such simple thing as "central participation" in a community of practice. Peripherality suggests that there are

35

multiple, varied, more- or less-engaged and -inclusive ways of being located in the fields of participation defined by a community. Peripheral participation is about being located in the social world. *Changing* locations and perspectives are part of actors' learning trajectories, developing identities, and forms of membership.

Furthermore, legitimate peripherality is a complex notion, implicated in social structures involving relations of power. As a place in which one moves toward more-intensive participation, peripherality is an empowering position. As a place in which one is kept from participating more fully – often legitimately, from the broader perspective of society at large – it is a disempowering position. Beyond that, legitimate peripherality can be a position at the articulation of related communities. In this sense, it can itself be a source of power or powerlessness, in affording or preventing articulation and interchange among communities of practice. The ambiguous potentialities of legitimate peripherality reflect the concept's pivotal role in providing access to a nexus of relations otherwise not perceived as connected.

Given the complex, differentiated nature of communities, it seems important not to reduce the end point of centripetal participation in a community of practice to a uniform or univocal "center," or to a linear notion of skill acquisition. There is no place in a community of practice designated "the periphery," and, most emphatically, it has no single core or center. *Central participation* would imply that there is a center (physical, political, or metaphorical) to a community with respect to an individual's "place" in it. *Complete participation* would suggest a closed domain of knowledge or collective practice for which there might be measurable degrees of "acquisition" by newcomers. We have chosen to call that to which peripheral

36

participation leads, *full participation*. Full participation is intended to do justice to the diversity of relations involved in
varying forms of community membership.

Full participation, however, stands in contrast to only one
aspect of the concept of peripherality as we see it: It places the
emphasis on what partial participation is not, or not yet. In our
usage, *peripherality* is also a *positive* term, whose most salient
conceptual antonyms are *unrelatedness* or *irrelevance* to ongoing activity. The partial participation of newcomers is by no
means "disconnected" from the practice of interest. Furthermore, it is also a dynamic concept. In this sense, peripherality,
when it is enabled, suggests an opening, a way of gaining
access to sources for understanding through growing involvement. The ambiguity inherent in peripheral participation must
then be connected to issues of legitimacy, of the social organization of and control over resources, if it is to gain its full
analytical potential.

AN ANALYTIC PERSPECTIVE ON LEARNING

With the first shift in the development of this project we have
tried to establish that our historical–cultural theory of learning
should not be merely an abstracted generalization of the concrete cases of apprenticeship – or any other educational form.
Further, coming to see that a theory of situated activity challenges the very meaning of abstraction and/or generalization
has led us to reject conventional readings of the generalizabil-
ity and/or abstraction of "knowledge." Arguing in favor of a
shift away from a theory of situated activity in which learning
is reified as one kind of activity, and toward a theory of social

37

practice in which learning is viewed as an aspect of all activity, has led us to consider how we are to think about our own practice. And this has revealed a dilemma: How can we purport to be working out a *theoretical conception* of learning without, in fact, engaging in just the project of abstraction rejected above?

There are several classical dualist oppositions that in many contexts are treated as synonymous, or nearly so: abstract–concrete; general–particular; theory about the world, and the world so described. Theory is assumed to be general and abstract, the world, concrete and particular. But in the Marxist historical tradition that underpins social practice theory these terms take on different relations with each other and different meanings. They do so as part of a general method of social analysis. This method does not deny that there is a concrete world, which is ordinarily perceived as some collection of particularities, just as it is possible to invent simple, thin, abstract theoretical propositions about it. But these two possibilities are not considered as the two poles of interest. Instead, both of them offer points of departure for starting to explore and produce an understanding of multiply determined, diversely unified – that is, complexly concrete – historical processes, of which particularities (including initial theories) are the result (Marx 1857; Hall 1973; Ilyenkov 1977). The theorist is trying to recapture those relations in an analytic way that turns the apparently "natural" categories and forms of social life into challenges to our understanding of how they are (historically and culturally) produced and reproduced. The goal, in Marx's memorable phrase, is to "ascend (from both the particular and the abstract) to the concrete."

It may now be clearer why it is not appropriate to treat legitimate peripheral participation as a mere distillation of apprenticeship, an abstracting process of generalizing from examples of apprenticeship. (Indeed, turned onto apprenticeship, the concept should provide the same analytical leverage as it would for any other educational form.) Our theorizing about legitimate peripheral participation thus is not intended as abstraction, but as an attempt to explore its concrete relations. To think about a concept like legitimate peripheral participation in this way is to argue that its theoretical significance derives from the richness of its interconnections: in historical terms, through time and across cultures. It may convey better what we mean by a historically, culturally concrete ''concept'' to describe legitimate peripheral participation as an ''analytical perspective.'' We use these two terms interchangeably hereafter.

WITH LEGITIMATE PERIPHERAL PARTICIPATION

We do not talk here about schools in any substantial way, nor explore what our work has to say about schooling. Steering clear of the problem of school learning for the present was a conscious decision, which was not always easy to adhere to as the issue kept creeping into our discussions. But, although we mention schooling at various points, we have refrained from any systematic treatment of the subject. It is worth outlining our reasons for this restraint, in part because this may help clarify further the theoretical status of the concept of legitimate peripheral participation.

First, as we began to focus on legitimate peripheral participation, we wanted above all to take a fresh look at learning. Issues of learning and schooling seemed to have become too deeply interrelated in our culture in general, both for purposes of our own exploration and the exposition of our ideas. More importantly, the organization of schooling as an educational form is predicated on claims that knowledge can be decontextualized, and yet schools themselves as social institutions and as places of learning constitute very specific contexts. Thus, analysis of school learning as situated requires a multilayered view of how knowing and learning are part of social practice – a major project in its own right. Last, but not least, pervasive claims concerning the sources of the effectiveness of schooling (in teaching, in the specialization of schooling in changing persons, in the special modes of inculcation for which schools are known) stand in contradiction with the situated perspective we have adopted. All this has meant that our discussions of schooling were often contrastive, even oppositional. But we did not want to define our thinking and build our theory primarily by contrast to the claims of any educational form, including schooling. We wanted to develop a view of learning that would stand on its own, reserving the analysis of schooling and other specific educational forms for the future.

We should emphasize, therefore, that legitimate peripheral participation is not itself an educational form, much less a pedagogical strategy or a teaching technique. It is an analytical viewpoint on learning, a way of understanding learning. We hope to make clear as we proceed that learning through legitimate peripheral participation takes place no matter which educational form provides a context for learning, or whether there is any intentional educational form at all. Indeed, this viewpoint makes a fundamental distinction between learning and intentional instruction. Such decoupling does not deny that learning can take place where there is teaching, but does not take intentional instruction to be in itself the source or cause of learning, and thus does not blunt the claim that what gets learned is problematic with respect to what is taught. Undoubtedly, the analytical perspective of legitimate peripheral participation could – we hope that it will – inform educational endeavors by shedding a new light on learning processes, and by drawing attention to key aspects of learning experience that may be overlooked. But this is very different from attributing a prescriptive value to the concept of legitimate peripheral participation and from proposing ways of "implementing" or "operationalizing" it for educational purposes.

Even though we decided to set aside issues of schooling in this initial stage of our work, we are persuaded that rethinking schooling from the perspective afforded by legitimate peripheral participation will turn out to be a fruitful exercise. Such an analysis would raise questions about the place of schooling in the community at large in terms of possibilities for developing identities of mastery. These include questions of the relation of school practices to those of the communities in which the knowledge that schools are meant to "impart" is located, as well as issues concerning relations between the world of schooling and the world of adults more generally. Such a study would also raise questions about the social organization of schools themselves into communities of practice, both official and interstitial, with varied forms of membership. We would predict that such an investigation would afford a better context for determining what students learn and what they do not, and what it comes to mean for them, than would a study of the curriculum or of instructional practices.

Thinking about schooling in terms of legitimate peripheral participation is only one of several directions that seem promising for pursuing the analysis of contemporary and other historical forms of social practice in terms of legitimate peripheral participation in communities of practice. There are central issues that are only touched upon in this monograph, and that need to be given more attention. The concept of "community of practice" is left largely as an intuitive notion, which serves a purpose here but which requires a more rigorous treatment. In particular, unequal relations of power must be included more systematically in our analysis. Hegemony over resources for learning and alienation from full participation are inherent in the shaping of the legitimacy and peripherality of participation in its historical realizations. It would be useful to understand better how these relations generate characteristically interstitial communities of practice and truncate possibilities for identities of mastery.

THE ORGANIZATION OF THIS MONOGRAPH

In this brief history we have tried to convey how and why the core concept of legitimate peripheral participation has taken on theoretical interest for us. In the next chapter we place this history in a broader theoretical context and investigate assumptions about learning; we contrast our own views to conventional views concerning internalization, the construction of identity, and the production of communities of practice. In Chapter 3, we present excerpts from five studies of apprenticeship, analyzing them as instances of learning through legitimate peripheral participation. These studies raise a series of issues: the relations between learning and pedagogy, the place of knowledge in practice, the importance of access to the learning potential of given settings, the uses of language in learning-in-practice, and the way in which knowledge takes on value for the learner in the fashioning of identities of full participation. Our discussion of these issues provokes an examination of the fundamental contradictions embodied in relations of legitimate peripheral participation, and of how such contradictions are involved in generating change (Chapter 4). In conclusion, we emphasize the significance of shifting the analytic focus from the individual as learner to learning as participation in the social world, and from the concept of cognitive process to the more-encompassing view of social practice.

2

Practice, Person,
Social World

Practice, Person, Social World

All theories of learning are based on fundamental assumptions about the person, the world, and their relations, and we have argued that this monograph formulates a theory of learning as a dimension of social practice. Indeed, the concept of legitimate peripheral participation provides a framework for bringing together theories of situated activity and theories about the production and reproduction of the social order. These have usually been treated separately, and within distinct theoretical traditions. But there is common ground for exploring their integral, constitutive relations, their entailments, and effects in a framework of social practice theory, in which the production, transformation, and change in the identities of persons, knowledgeable skill in practice, and communities of practice are realized in the lived-in world of engagement in everyday activity.

INTERNALIZATION OF THE CULTURAL GIVEN

Conventional explanations view learning as a process by which a learner internalizes knowledge, whether "discovered," "transmitted" from others, or "experienced in interaction" with others. This focus on internalization does not just leave the nature of the learner, of the world, and of their relations unexplored; it can only reflect far-reaching assumptions concerning these issues. It establishes a sharp dichotomy between inside and outside, suggests that knowledge is largely cerebral, and takes the individual as the nonproblematic unit of analysis. Furthermore, learning as internalization is too easily construed as an unproblematic process of absorbing the given, as a matter of transmission and assimilation.

47

Situated Learning

Internalization is even central to some work on learning explicitly concerned with its social character, for instance in the work of Vygotsky. We are aware that Vygotsky's concept of the zone of proximal development has received vastly differing interpretations, under which the concept of internalization plays different roles. These interpretations can be roughly classified into three categories. First, the zone of proximal development is often characterized as the distance between problem-solving abilities exhibited by a learner working alone and that learner's problem-solving abilities when assisted by or collaborating with more-experienced people. This "scaffolding" interpretation has inspired pedagogical approaches that explictly provide support for the initial performance of tasks to be later performed without assistance (Greenfield 1984; Wood, Bruner, and Ross 1976; for critiques of this position, see Engeström 1987, and Griffin and Cole 1984). Second, a "cultural" interpretation construes the zone of proximal development as the distance between thc cultural knowledge provided by the sociohistorical context – usually made accessible through instruction – and the everyday experience of individuals (Davydov and Markova 1983). Hedegaard (1988) calls this the distance between understood knowledge, as provided by instruction, and active knowledge, as owned by individuals. This interpretation is based on Vygotsky's distinction between scientific and everyday concepts, and on his argument that a mature concept is achieved when the scientific and everyday versions have merged. In these two classes of interpretation of the concept of the zone of proximal development, the social character of learning mostly consists in a small "aura" of socialness that provides input for the process of internalization viewed as individualistic acquisition of the cultural given. There is no account of the place of learning in the broader context of the structure of the social world (Fajans and Turner in preparation).

Contemporary developments in the traditions of Soviet psychology, in which Vygotsky's work figures prominently, include activity theory (Bakhurst 1988; Engeström 1987; Wertsch 1981, 1985) and critical psychology (Holzkamp 1983, 1987; Dreier in press; see also Garner 1986). In the context of these recent developments, a third type of interpretation of the zone of proximal development takes a "collectivist," or "societal" perspective. Engeström defines the zone of proximal development as the "distance between the everyday actions of individuals and the historically new form of the societal activity that can be collectively generated as a solution to the double bind potentially embedded in . . . everyday actions" (Engeström 1987: 174). Under such societal interpretations of the concept of the zone of proximal development researchers tend to concentrate on processes of social transformation. They share our interest in extending the study of learning beyond the context of pedagogical structuring, including the structure of the social world in the analysis, and taking into account in a central way the conflictual nature of social practice. We place more emphasis on connecting issues of sociocultural transformation with the changing relations between newcomers and old-timers in the context of a changing shared practice.

PARTICIPATION IN SOCIAL PRACTICE

In contrast with learning as internalization, learning as increasing participation in communities of practice concerns the whole person acting in the world. Conceiving of learning in terms of

49

participation focuses attention on ways in which it is an evolving, continuously renewed set of relations; this is, of course,
consistent with a relational view, of persons, their actions, and
the world, typical of a theory of social practice.

Theorizing about social practice, praxis, activity, and the
development of human knowing through participation in an
ongoing social world is part of a long Marxist tradition in the
social sciences. It influences us most immediately through
contemporary anthropological and sociological theorizing about
practice. The critique of structural and phenomenological theory early in Bourdieu's *Outline of a Theory of Practice*, with
its vision of conductorless orchestras, and regulation without
rules, embodied practices and cultural dispositions concerted
in class habitus, suggest the possibility of a (crucially important) break with the dualisms that have kept persons reduced
to their minds, mental processes to instrumental rationalism,
and learning to the acquisition of knowledge (the discourse of
dualism effectively segregates even these reductions from the
everyday world of engaged participation). Insistence on the
historical nature of motivation, desire, and the very relations
by which social and culturally mediated experience is available to persons-in-practice is one key to the goals to be met in
developing a theory of practice. Theorizing in terms of practice, or praxis, also requires a broad view of human agency
(e.g., Giddens 1979), emphasizing the integration in practice
of agent, world, and activity (Bourdieu 1977; Ortner 1984;
Bauman 1973).

Briefly, a theory of social practice emphasizes the relational
interdependency of agent and world, activity, meaning, cognition, learning, and knowing. It emphasizes the inherently
socially negotiated character of meaning and the interested,
concerned character of the thought and action of persons-in-

activity. This view also claims that learning, thinking, and knowing are relations among people in activity in, with, and arising from the socially and culturally structured world. This world is socially constituted; objective forms and systems of activity, on the one hand, and agents' subjective and intersubjective understandings of them, on the other, mutually constitute both the world and its experienced forms. Knowledge of the socially constituted world is socially mediated and open ended. Its meaning to given actors, its furnishings, and the relations of humans with/in it, are produced, reproduced, and changed in the course of activity (which includes speech and thought, but cannot be reduced to one or the other). In a theory of practice, cognition and communication in, and with, the social world are situated in the historical development of ongoing activity. It is, thus, a critical theory; the social scientist's practice must be analyzed in the same historical, situated terms as any other practice under investigation. One way to think of learning is as the historical production, transformation, and change of persons. Or to put it the other way around, in a thoroughly historical theory of social practice, the historicizing of the production of persons should lead to a focus on processes of learning.

Let us return to the question of internalization from such a relational perspective. First, the historicizing of processes of learning gives the lie to ahistorical views of "internalization" as a universal process. Further, given a relational understanding of person, world, and activity, participation, at the core of our theory of learning, can be neither fully internalized as knowledge structures nor fully externalized as instrumental artifacts or overarching activity structures. Participation is always based on situated negotiation and renegotiation of meaning in the world. This implies that understanding and experience

51

are in constant interaction – indeed, are mutually constitutive. The notion of participation thus dissolves dichotomies between cerebral and embodied activity, between contemplation and involvement, between abstraction and experience: persons, actions, and the world are implicated in all thought, speech, knowing, and learning.

THE PERSON AND IDENTITY IN LEARNING

Our claim, that focusing on the structure of social practice and on participation therein implies an explicit focus on the person, may appear paradoxical at first. The individualistic aspects of the cognitive focus characteristic of most theories of learning thus only seem to concentrate on the person. Painting a picture of the person as a primarily "cognitive" entity tends to promote a nonpersonal view of knowledge, skills, tasks, activities, and learning. As a consequence, both theoretical analyses and instructional prescriptions tend to be driven by reference to reified "knowledge domains," and by constraints imposed by the general requirements of universal learning mechanisms understood in terms of acquisition and assimilation. In contrast, to insist on starting with social practice, on taking participation to be the crucial process, and on including the social world at the core of the analysis only seems to eclipse the person. In reality, however, participation in social practice – subjective as well as objective – suggests a very explicit focus on the person, but as person-in-the-world, as member of a sociocultural community. This focus in turn promotes a view of knowing as activity by specific people in specific circumstances.

Practice, Person, Social World

As an aspect of social practice, learning involves the whole person; it implies not only a relation to specific activities, but a relation to social communities – it implies becoming a full participant, a member, a kind of person. In this view, learning only partly – and often incidentally – implies becoming able to be involved in new activities, to perform new tasks and functions, to master new understandings. Activities, tasks, functions, and understandings do not exist in isolation; they are part of broader systems of relations in which they have meaning. These systems of relations arise out of and are reproduced and developed within social communities, which are in part systems of relations among persons. The person is defined by as well as defines these relations. Learning thus implies becoming a different person with respect to the possibilities enabled by these systems of relations. To ignore this aspect of learning is to overlook the fact that learning involves the construction of identities.

Viewing learning as legitimate peripheral participation means that learning is not merely a condition for membership, but is itself an evolving form of membership. We conceive of identities as long-term, living relations between persons and their place and participation in communities of practice. Thus identity, knowing, and social membership entail one another.

There may seem to be a contradiction between efforts to "decenter" the definition of the person and efforts to arrive at a rich notion of agency in terms of "whole persons." We think that the two tendencies are not only compatible but that they imply one another, if one adopts as we have a relational view of the person and of learning: It is by the theoretical process of decentering in relational terms that one can construct a robust notion of "whole person" which does justice to the multiple relations through which persons define themselves in

53

practice. Giddens (1979) argues for a view of decentering that avoids the pitfalls of "structural determination" by considering intentionality as an ongoing flow of reflective moments of monitoring in the context of engagement in a tacit practice. We argue further that this flow of reflective moments is organized around trajectories of participation. This implies that changing membership in communities of practice, like participation, can be neither fully internalized nor fully externalized.

THE SOCIAL WORLD

If participation in social practice is the fundamental form of learning, we require a more fully worked-out view of the social world. Typically, theories, when they are concerned with the situated nature of learning at all, address its sociocultural character by considering only its immediate context. For instance, the activity of children learning is often presented as located in instructional environments and as occurring in the context of pedagogical intentions whose context goes unanalyzed. But there are several difficulties here, some of which will be discussed later when we address the traditional connection of learning to instruction.

Of concern here is an absence of theorizing about the social world as it is implicated in processes of learning. We think it is important to consider how shared cultural systems of meaning and political–economic structuring are interrelated, in general and as they help to coconstitute learning in communities of practice. "Locating" learning in classroom interaction is not an adequate substitute for a theory about what schooling as an activity system has to do with learning. Nor is a theory of the sociohistorical structuring of schooling (or simple extrapolations from it) adequate to account for other kinds of communities and the forms of legitimate peripheral participation therein. Another difficulty is that the classroom, or the school, or schooling (the context of learning activity cannot be unambiguously identified with one of these while excluding the other two) does not exist alone, but conventional theories of learning do not offer a means for grasping their interrelations. In effect, they are more concerned with furnishing the immediate social environment of the target action/interaction than with theorizing about the broader forces shaping and being shaped by those more immediate relations.

To furnish a more adequate account of the social world of learning in practice, we need to specify the analytic units and questions that would guide such a project. Legitimate peripheral participation refers both to the development of knowledgeably skilled identities in practice and to the reproduction and transformation of communities of practice. It concerns the latter insofar as communities of practice consist of and depend on a membership, including its characteristic biographies/trajectories, relationships, and practices.

Legitimate peripheral participation is intended as a conceptual bridge – as a claim about the common processes inherent in the production of changing persons and changing communities of practice. This pivotal emphasis, via legitimate peripheral participation, on relations between the production of knowledgeable identities and the production of communities of practice, makes it possible to think of sustained learning as embodying, albeit in transformed ways, the structural characteristics of communities of practice. This in turn raises questions about the sociocultural organization of space into places of activity and the circulation of knowledgeable skill; about the structure of access of learners to ongoing activity and the transparency of technology, social relations, and forms of activity; about the segmentation, distribution, and coordination of participation and the legitimacy of partial, increasing, changing participation within a community; about its characteristic conflicts, interests, common meanings, and intersecting interpretations and the motivation of all participants vis à vis their changing participation and identities – issues, in short, about the structure of communities of practice and their production and reproduction.

In any given concrete community of practice the process of community reproduction – a historically constructed, ongoing, conflicting, synergistic structuring of activity and relations among practitioners – must be deciphered in order to understand specific forms of legitimate peripheral participation through time. This requires a broader conception of individual and collective biographies than the single segment encompassed in studies of "learners." Thus we have begun to analyze the changing forms of participation and identity of persons who engage in sustained participation in a community of practice: from entrance as a newcomer, through becoming an old-timer with respect to new newcomers, to a point when those newcomers themselves become old-timers. Rather than a teacher/learner dyad, this points to a richly diverse field of essential actors and, with it, other forms of relationships of participation.

For example, in situations where learning-in-practice takes the form of apprenticeship, succeeding generations of participants give rise to what in its simplest form is a triadic set of relations: The community of practice encompasses apprentices, young masters with apprentices, and masters some of whose apprentices have themselves become masters. But there are other inflection points as well, where journeyfolk, not yet masters, are *relative* old-timers with respect to newcomers. The diversified field of relations among old-timers and new-comers within and across the various cycles, and the importance of near-peers in the circulation of knowledgeable skill, both recommend against assimilating relations of learning to the dyadic form characteristic of conventional learning studies.

Among the insights that can be gained from a social perspective on learning is the problematic character of processes of learning and cycles of social reproduction, as well as the relations between the two. These cycles emerge in the contradictions and struggles inherent in social practice and the formation of identities. There is a fundamental contradiction in the meaning to newcomers and old-timers of increasing participation by the former; for the centripetal development of full participants, and with it the successful production of a community of practice, also implies the *replacement* of old-timers. This contradiction is inherent in learning viewed as legitimate peripheral participation, albeit in various forms, since competitive relations, in the organization of production or in the formation of identities, clearly intensify these tensions.

One implication of the inherently problematic character of the social reproduction of communities of practice is that the sustained participation of newcomers, becoming old-timers, must involve conflict between the forces that support processes of learning and those that work against them. Another related implication is that learning is never simply a process of transfer or assimilation: Learning, transformation, and change are always implicated in one another, and the status quo needs as much explanation as change. Indeed, we must not forget that communities of practice are engaged in the generative process of producing their own future. Because of the contradictory nature of collective social practice and because learning processes are part of the working out of these contradictions in practice, social reproduction implies the renewed construction of resolutions to underlying conflicts. In this regard, it is important to note that reproduction cycles are productive as well. They leave a historical trace of artifacts – physical, linguistic, and symbolic – and of social structures, which constitute and reconstitute the practice over time.

The following chapter begins the exploration of legitimate peripheral participation with a description of apprenticeship in five communities of practice and their location in relation to other structuring forms and forces. These studies raise – at one and the same time – questions about persons acting and the social world in relation to which they act. The questions focus on relations between forms of production and the reproduction of communities of practice, on the one hand, and the production of persons, knowledgeable skill, and identities of mastery, on the other.

3

Midwives, Tailors, Quartermasters, Butchers, Nondrinking Alcoholics

Midwives, Tailors, Quartermasters, Butchers, Alcoholics

Actual cases of apprenticeship provide historically and culturally specific examples which seem especially helpful in exploring the implications of the concept of legitimate peripheral participation. As we have insisted, however, the concept should not be construed as a distillation of apprenticeship. Ethnographic studies of apprenticeship emphasize the indivisible character of learning and work practices. This, in turn, helps to make obvious the social nature of learning and knowing. As these studies partially illustrate, any complex system of work and learning has roots in and interdependencies across its history, technology, developing work activity, careers, and the relations between newcomers and old-timers and among co-workers and practitioners.

We have already outlined some reasons for turning away from schooling in our search for exemplary material, though schooling provides the empirical basis for much cognitive research on learning and also for much work based on the notion of the zone of proximal development. Such research is conceptually tied in various ways to school instruction and to the pedagogical intentions of teachers and other caregivers. In this context, schooling is usually assumed to be a more effective and advanced institution for educational transmission than (supposedly) previous forms such as apprenticeship. At the very least, schooling is given a privileged role in intellectual development. Because the theory and the institution have common historical roots (Lave 1988), these school-forged theories are inescapably specialized: They are unlikely to afford us the historical–cultural breadth to which we aspire. It seems useful, given these concerns, to investigate learning-in-practice in situations that do not draw us in unreflective ways into the school milieu, and to look for ''educational'' occasions whose structure is not obscured quite so profoundly as those founded on didactic structuring.

THE CASE OF APPRENTICESHIP

For present purposes, we have gathered together examples of apprenticeship from different cultural and historical traditions. This process clearly requires us to assume the validity of applying such a rubric across widely disparate times and places. It is not our intention to carry out here the searching examination that this assumption requires, though we would be glad to see our use of it get such a discussion under way. Meanwhile, since we found it useful to investigate the common, readily identifiable features of apprenticeship in craft or "craftlike" forms of production and to push toward the commonsense boundaries of the concept with our choice of examples, a brief foray into the controversies surrounding the concept of apprenticeship is in order.

The historical significance of apprenticeship as a form for producing knowledgeably skilled persons has been overlooked, we believe, for it does not conform to either functionalist or Marxist views of educational "progress." In both traditions apprenticeship has been treated as a historically significant object more often than most educational phenomena – but only to emphasize its anachronistic irrelevance. It connotes both outmoded production and obsolete education. When its history is the pretext for dismissing an issue as an object of study, there is good reason to reexamine its existing historical and cultural diversity.

We take issue with a narrow reading of apprenticeship as if

it were always and everywhere organized in the same ways as in feudal Europe. Engeström, for instance, associates apprenticeship with craft production, emphasizing the individual or small-group nature of production, the use of simple tools and tacit knowledge, a division of labor based on individual adaptation, and the prevalence of traditional protective codes (1987: 284). But this does not fit the descriptions of apprenticeship presented here. In fact, we emphasize the diversity of historical forms, cultural traditions, and modes of production in which apprenticeship is found (in contrast with research that stresses the uniform effects of schooling regardless of its location).

Forms of apprenticeship have been described for, among other historical traditions, ancient China; Europe, feudal and otherwise; and much of the contemporary world including West Africa and the United States (e.g., Goody 1982; Coy 1989; Cooper 1980; Geer 1972; Jordan 1989; Medick 1976). In the United States today much learning occurs in the form of some sort of apprenticeship, especially wherever high levels of knowledge and skill are in demand (e.g., medicine, law, the academy, professional sports, and the arts). The examples presented below come from different cultural traditions that have emerged in different periods in their separate and related histories in different parts of the world. All are contemporary and each reflects the complex articulation of modes of production in which it is embedded. Our intention is to show how learning or failure to learn in each of our examples of apprenticeship may be accounted for by underlying relations of legitimate peripheral participation.

In a useful caution to recent enthusiasm about the efficacy of apprenticeship learning, Grosshans (1989) points out that in Western Europe and indeed in the United States (where its renewal in the 1920s and 1930s served as a convenient means of exploiting workers), apprenticeship has a long reputation as a traditional form of control over the most valuable, least powerful workers. In contemporary West Africa, however, for complex reasons, among them the poverty, large numbers, and unorganized state of craft masters, there appears to be a relatively benign, relatively egalitarian, and nonexploitive character to apprenticeship. There is no point, then, either in damning apprenticeship absolutely, on the basis of its sorry reputation in Western Europe, or in glorifying it unreflectively. Although apprenticeship has no determined balance of relations of power as an abstract concept, it does have such relations in every concrete case. Any given attempt to analyze a form of learning through legitimate peripheral participation must involve analysis of the political and social organization of that form, its historical development, and the effects of both of these on sustained possibilities for learning.

The need for such analysis motivates our focus on communities of practice and our insistence that learners must be legitimate peripheral participants in ongoing practice in order for learning identities to be engaged and develop into full participation. Conditions that place newcomers in deeply adversarial relations with masters, bosses, or managers; in exhausting overinvolvement in work; or in involuntary servitude rather than participation distort, partially or completely, the prospects for learning in practice. Our viewpoint suggests that communities of practice may well develop interstitially and informally in coercive workplaces. What will be learned then will be the sociocultural practices of whatever informal community takes place in response to coercion (Orr in press). These practices shape and are shaped indirectly through resistance to the prescriptions of the ostensibly primary organizational form.

Midwives, Tailors, Quartermasters, Butchers, Alcoholics

FIVE STUDIES OF APPRENTICESHIP

We present excerpts from five accounts of apprenticeship: among Yucatec Mayan midwives in Mexico (Jordan 1989), among Vai and Gola tailors in Liberia (Lave in preparation), in the work-learning settings of U.S. navy quartermasters (Hutchins in press), among butchers in U.S. supermarkets (Marshall 1972), and among "nondrinking alcoholics" in Alcoholics Anonymous (Cain n.d.). Even though this last case is not usually described as a form of apprenticeship, the learning this study describes is so remarkably similar to the first four in its basic character that it serves to highlight common features of the others.

These studies illustrate the varied character of concrete realizations of apprenticeship. But it is noteworthy that all of them diverge in similar ways from popular stereotypes about apprenticeship learning. It is typically assumed, for example, that apprenticeship has had an exclusive existence in association with feudal craft production; that master–apprentice relations are diagnostic of apprenticeship; and that learning in apprenticeship offers opportunities for nothing more complex than reproducing task performances in routinized ways. The cases also call into question assumptions that learning through apprenticeship shows some typical degree of informal organization.

The first three cases, as well as the last, are quite effective forms of learning; the fourth – butchers' apprenticeship in contemporary supermarkets – often doesn't work. The technologies employed, the forms of recruitment, the relations between masters and apprentices, and the organization of learning activity differ. The Yucatec midwives provide healing and ritual services using herbal remedies, their knowledge of techniques of birthing (including a manual cephalic version to prevent breech births), massage, and ritual procedures. The tailors are engaged in craft production for the market, using simple technology (e.g., scissors, measuring tape, thread and needle, and treadle sewing machines); masters work individually, assisted only by their apprentices. The quartermasters utilize high technology in "knowledge production" involving telescopic sighting devices called *alidades,* radio telephones, maps and nautical charts, a logbook, plotting devices, and collaborative labor. The butchers perform a commoditized service (meat cutting) using powered cutting tools and plastic-wrapping machines. And the members of A. A. band together to cope with what they perceive to be an incurable disease.

Apprentice Yucatec midwives (all women) are almost always the daughters of experienced midwives – specialized knowledge and practice is passed down within families. In the case of the tailors (all men), the apprentice and his family negotiate with a master tailor to take a newcomer into his house and family and make sure he learns the craft. The master is rarely a close relative of the apprentice. Quartermasters leave home to join the Navy, and become part of that total institution for a relatively short period of time (two or three years). They have "instructors" and "officers" and work with other "enlisted persons." Butchers' apprentices join a union and are placed in trade schools; they receive on-the-job training in supermarkets, where they are supposed to learn meat cutting from the master butchers and journeymen who work there. A. A. members join the organization, attend frequent meetings, and gradually adopt a view of themselves, through their membership in A. A., which becomes an integral part of their life. The butchers and in some respects the quartermasters are wage laborers; the midwives and tailors' apprentices, and of course A. A. members, are not.

There is variation in the forms of apprenticeship and the degree of integration of apprenticeship into daily life, as well as in the forms of production with which apprenticeship is associated. For instance, apprenticeship is not always, or perhaps even often, "informal." For midwives in Yucatan, apprenticeship is integrated into daily life and it is only recognized after the fact that they have served an apprenticeship. They describe the process as one in which they receive their calling and learn everything they know in dreams, though they are middle-aged adepts when this happens (Jordan 1989: 933). On the other hand, Vai masters and apprentices enter into a formal agreement before apprenticeship begins, there is some explicit structure to the learning curriculum, apprenticeship *is* their daily life, and at the close of the apprenticeship the new master must receive the official blessing of his master before he can begin a successful business independently. Quartermasters enter training programs and receive certificates, as do butchers. The apprenticeship of nondrinking alcoholics is sanctified by an explicit commitment to the organization and passage through well-defined "steps" of membership.

THE APPRENTICESHIP OF YUCATEC MIDWIVES

Jordan (1989) describes the process by which Yucatec midwives move, over a period of many years, from peripheral to full participation in midwifery. This work poses a puzzle concerning the general role of masters in the lives of apprentices. Teaching does not seem to be central either to the identities of master midwives or to learning.

Apprenticeship happens as a way of, and in the course of, daily life. It may not be recognized as a teaching effort at all. A Maya girl who eventually becomes a midwife most likely has a mother or grandmother who is a midwife, since midwifery is handed down in family lines. . . . Girls in such families, without being identified as apprentice midwives, absorb the essence of midwifery practice as well as specific knowledge about many procedures, simply in the process of growing up. They know what the life of a midwife is like (for example, that she needs to go out at all hours of the day or night), what kinds of stories the women and men who come to consult her tell, what kinds of herbs and other remedies need to be collected, and the like. As young children they might be sitting quietly in a corner as their mother administers a prenatal massage; they would hear stories of difficult cases, of miraculous outcomes, and the like. As they grow older, they may be passing messages, running errands, getting needed supplies. A young girl might be present as her mother stops for a postpartum visit after the daily shopping trip to the market.

Eventually, after she has had a child herself, she might come along to a birth, perhaps because her ailing grandmother needs someone to walk with, and thus find herself doing for the woman in labor what other women had done for her when she gave birth; that is, she may take a turn . . . at supporting the laboring woman. . . . Eventually, she may even administer prenatal massages to selected clients. At some point, she may decide that she actually wants to do this kind of work. She then pays more attention, but only rarely does she ask questions. Her mentor sees their association primarily as one that is of some use to her. ("Rosa already knows how to do a massage, so I can send her if I am too busy.") As time goes on, the apprentice takes over more and more of the work load, starting with the routine and tedious parts, and ending with what is in Yucatan the culturally most significant, the birth of the placenta [Jordan 1989: 932–4].

THE APPRENTICESHIP OF VAI AND GOLA TAILORS

Vai and Gola tailors enter and leave apprenticeship ceremoniously. Their apprenticeship is quite formal in character compared to that of the Yucatec midwives. In an insightful historical analysis, Goody (1989) argues that in West Africa apprenticeship developed a formal character in response to a diversification of the division of labor. This development involved a transition from domestic production in which children learned subsistence skills from their same-sex parent, to learning part-time specialisms in the same way, to learning a specialized occupation from a specialist master. Household production units have moved from integrating their own children into productive activities, to including other kin, to incorporating nonkin, to production separated from the household. Today, many Vai and Gola craft shops are located in commercial areas, so that craft production is separated from craft masters' households by time and space. (These households, however, still include the apprentices who work in the shops.) Goody notes that there have been corresponding transformations in the relations between learners and communities of practice: from the child's labor that contributes use value to the household, to exchange of child labor between related families for political/social resources (fostering) or economic ones (pawning, slavery), to apprenticeship where learners' labor is exchanged for opportunities to learn. Learning to produce has changed thereby from a process of general socialization; to what might be called contrastive general socialization (as children grow up in households different from their own); to apprenticeship, which focuses on occupational specialization loosely within the context of household socialization. Learners shifted from participating in the division of labor as household members, growing up in the "culture of the household's labor," to being naive newcomers, participating in an unfamiliar culture of production.

In summary, formalized apprenticeship in West Africa has developed as a mechanism for dealing with two needs generated by increasing diversification of the market and of the division of labor: the demand for additional labor, on the one hand, and on the other, the desires of individuals or families to acquire the knowledgeable skills of diverse occupations, desires which simply could not be met within the household (Goody 1989). The developmental cycles that reproduce domestic groups and other communities of practice, the relations of newcomers to those who are adept, and the way in which divisions of labor articulate various kinds of communities of practice in communities in the larger sense all shape the identities that may be constructed, and with them, knowledgeable, skillful activity. Nonetheless, the examples of the midwives and the tailors reveal strong similarities in the process of moving from peripheral to full participation in communities of practice through either formal or informal apprenticeship.

> Between 1973 and 1978 . . . a number of Vai and Gola tailors clustered their wood, dirt-floored, tin-roofed tailor shops along a narrow path at the edge of the river at the periphery of . . . the commercial district. . . . There were several masters present in each shop visibly doing what masters do – each ran a business, tailored clothes, and supervised apprentices. Apprenticeship, averaging five years, involved a sustained, rich structure of opportunities to observe masters, journeymen, and other apprentices at work, to observe frequently the full process of producing garments, and of course, the finished products.
>
> The tailors made clothes for the poorest segment of the population, and their specialty was inexpensive, ready-to-wear men's trousers. But they made other things as well. The list of garment types in fact encoded complex, intertwined forms of order integral to the process of becoming a master tailor [serving as a general "curriculum" for apprentices]. . . . Apprentices first learn to make hats and drawers, informal and intimate garments for children. They move on to more external, formal garments, ending with the Higher Heights suit.
>
> The organization of the process of apprenticeship is not confined to the level of whole garments. The very earliest steps in the process involve learning to sew by hand, to sew with the treadle sewing machine, and to press clothes. Subtract these from the corpus of tailor-

ing knowledge and for each garment the apprentice
must learn how to cut it out and how to sew it. Learning processes do not merely reproduce the sequence of
production processes. In fact, production steps are re-
versed, as apprentices begin by learning the finishing
stages of producing a garment, go on to learn to sew
it, and only later learn to cut it out. This pattern regu-
larly subdivides [the learning of] each new type of
garment. Reversing production steps has the effect of
focusing the apprentices' attention first on the broad
outlines of garment construction as they handle garments while attaching buttons and hemming cuffs. Next,
sewing turns their attention to the logic (order, orientation) by which different pieces are sewn together,
which in turn explains why they are cut out as they
are. Each step offers the unstated opportunity to consider how the previous step contributes to the present
one. In addition, this ordering minimizes experiences
of failure and especially of serious failure.

There is one further level of organization to the curriculum of tailoring. The learning of each operation is
subdivided into phases I have dubbed ''way-in'' and
''practice.'' ''Way in'' refers to the period of observation and attempts to construct a first approximation
of the garment. . . . The practice phase is carried out
in a particular way: apprentices reproduce a production segment from beginning to end, . . . though they
might be more skilled at carrying out some parts of the
process than others [Lave in preparation].

Midwives, Tailors, Quartermasters, Butchers, Alcoholics

THE APPRENTICESHIP OF NAVAL
QUARTERMASTERS

Hutchins (in press) has carried out ethnographic research on
an amphibious helicopter-transport ship of the U.S. Navy. He
describes the process by which new members of the quartermaster corps move from peripheral to key distributed tasks in
the collaborative work of plotting the ship's position. He emphasizes the importance for learning of having legitimate, effective access to what is to be learned.

> Quartermasters begin their careers with rather limited
> duties and advance to more complicated procedures as
> they gain expertise. . . . Any new quartermaster needs
> to learn to plot the ship's position, either alone when
> at sea, or in collaborative work with five others when
> moving into harbors. It takes about a year to learn the
> basics of the quartermaster rate. For a young man en-
> tering the quartermaster rate, there are many sources
> of information about the work to be done. Some go to
> specialized schools before they join a ship. There they
> are exposed to basic terminology and concepts, but
> little more. In some sense, they are "trained" but they
> have no experience. (In fact, the two quartermaster
> chiefs with whom I worked most closely said they pre-
> ferred to get their trainees as able-bodied seamen with-
> out any prior training in the rate. They said this saved
> them the trouble of having to break the trainees of bad
> habits acquired in school.) Most quartermasters learn
> their rating primarily on the job [though] some of the
> experience aboard ship is a bit like school with work-
> books and exercises. In order to advance to higher ranks

73

. . . novice quartermasters participate in joint activity with more experienced colleagues in two contexts: Standard Steaming Watch and Sea and Anchor Detail.

[At sea] depending upon the level of experience of the novice he may be asked to perform all of the duties of the quartermaster of the watch. While under instruction, his activities are closely monitored by the more experienced watch stander who is always on hand and can help out or take over if the novice is unable to satisfy the ship's navigation requirements. However, even with the help of a more experienced colleague, standing watch under instruction requires a significant amount of knowledge, so novices do not do this until they have several months of experience. . . . The task for the novice is to learn to organize his own behavior such that it produces a competent performance. . . . As [the novice] becomes more competent, he will do both the part of this task that he [performed before], and also the organizing part that was done [for him]. . . . Long before they are ready to stand watch under instruction in standard steaming watch, novice quartermasters begin to work as fathometer operators and bearing takers in sea and anchor detail; . . . there are six positions involved, and novice quartermasters move through this sequence of positions, mastering each before moving on to the next. This ordering also describes the flow of information from the sensors (fathometer and sighting telescopes) to the chart where the information is integrated into a single representation (the position fix). . . . The fact that the quartermasters themselves follow this same trajectory through the system as does sensed information, albeit on a different time scale, has an important consequence for the larger system's ability to detect, diagnose, and correct errors. . . . [Besides], movement through the system with increasing expertise results in a pattern of overlapping expertise, with knowledge of the entry level tasks most redundantly represented and knowledge of expert level tasks least redundantly represented.

 . . . The structure of the distributed task [fix taking among the collaborating six quartermasters] provides many constraints on the learning environment. The way a task is partitioned across a set of task performers has consequences for both the efficiency of task performance and for the efficiency of knowledge acquisition. . . . [So do] lines of communication and limits on observation of the activities of others. . . . But being in the presence of others who are working is not always enough by itself. . . . We saw that the fact that the work was done in an interaction between members opened it to other members of the team. In a similar way, the design of tools can affect their suitability for joint use. . . . The interaction of a task performer with a tool may or may not be open to others depending upon the nature of the tool itself. The openness of a tool can also affect its use as an instrument in instruction.

A good deal of the structure that a novice will have to acquire in order to stand watch alone in standard steaming watch is present in the organization of the relations among the members of the team in sea and anchor detail. The computational dependencies among

the steps of the procedure for the individual watch
stander are present as interpersonal dependencies among
the members of the team [Hutchins in press].

THE APPRENTICESHIP OF MEAT CUTTERS

Our use of apprenticeship as a source of insights for exploring
the concept of legitimate peripheral participation cannot be
construed as a general claim that apprenticeship facilitates
learning-in-practice in some inevitable way. Not all concrete
realizations of apprenticeship learning are equally effective.
The exchange of labor for opportunities to become part of a
community of mature practice is fraught with difficulties (Becker
1972). The commoditization of labor can transform apprentices into a cheap source of unskilled labor, put to work in
ways that deny them access to activities in the arenas of mature
practice. Gaining legitimacy may be so difficult that some fail
to learn until considerable time has passed. For example, Haas
(1972) describes how high-steel-construction apprentices are
hazed so roughly by old-timers that learning is inhibited. Gaining legitimacy is also a problem when masters prevent learning
by acting in effect as pedagogical authoritarians, viewing apprentices as novices who ''should be instructed'' rather than
as peripheral participants in a community engaged in its own
reproduction.

The example of the butchers illustrates several of the potential ways in which particular forms of apprenticeship can prevent rather than facilitate learning. The author discusses the
effects, frequently negative, of trade-school training for butchers. This study, like other studies of trade schools and training

76

programs in the apprenticeship literature, is quite pessimistic about the value of didactic exercises (e.g., Jordan 1989, Orr 1986, as well as the excerpt from Hutchins). It should be kept in mind that many contemporary vocational education and union-based "apprenticeship" programs implicitly reject an apprenticeship model and strive to approximate the didactic mode of schooling in their educational programs, which inevitably adds to the difficulties of implementing effective apprenticeship.

> Butchers' apprenticeship consists of a mix of trade school and on the job training. [This program was] started by the meat cutters' union to grant a certificate. The certificate equaled six months of the apprenticeship and entitled the holder to receive journeyman's pay and status after two and one-half years on the job. . . . To justify awarding the certificate, the trade school class runs in traditional fashion, with book work and written examinations in class and practice in shop. The work follows the same pattern year after year without reference to apprentices' need to learn useful things not learned on the job. Teachers teach techniques in use when they worked in retail markets that are readily adaptable to a school setting. . . . Most assignments are not relevant to the supermarket. For instance, students learn to make wholesale cuts not used in stores, or to advise customers in cooking meat. Because these are not skills in demand, few students bother to learn them. . . . Apprentices are more interested in the shop period, where they become familiar with equipment they hope to use someday at work. But the shop, too, has tasks useless in a supermarket. One of the first things learned is how to sharpen a knife – a vital task

only in the past. Today, a company delivers sharpened knives and collects dull ones from meat departments at regular intervals. . . .

On the job, learning experiences vary with certain structural dimensions of the work settings. A supermarket meat department manager tries to achieve an advantageous difference between the total volume of sales for the department and the wholesale price of his meat order, plus his costs for personnel and facilities. To do this, the manager sees to it that his skilled journeymen can prepare a large volume of meat efficiently by specializing in short, repetitive tasks. He puts apprentices where they can work for him most efficiently. Diverting journeymen from work to training tasks increases the short-run cost of selling meat. Because journeymen and apprentices are so occupied with profit-making tasks, apprentices rarely learn many tasks. . . .

The physical layout of a work setting is an important dimension of learning, since apprentices get a great deal from observing others and being observed. Some meat departments were laid out so that apprentices working at the wrapping machine could not watch journeymen cut and saw meat. An apprentice's feeling about this separation came out when a district manager in a large, local market told him to return poorly arranged trays of meat to the journeymen. "I'm scared to go in the back room. I feel so out of place there. I haven't gone back there in a long time because I just don't know what to do when I'm there. All those guys know so much about meat cutting and I don't know anything."

When he arrives at a store, an apprentice is trained to perform a task, usually working the automatic wrapping machine. If he handles this competently, he is kept there until another apprentice comes. If none comes, he may do this job for years almost without interruption. If a new apprentice comes, he trains him to wrap and then learns another task himself. . . . Stores offer the kind of meat customers in their locale will buy. . . . In poor neighborhoods, apprentices have more opportunity to practice cutting meat than in wealthy neighborhoods [due to lower error cost]. [Where there is high volume] a division of labor among a relatively large number of workers increases efficiency. . . . In this situation, not only apprentices but journeymen, too, seldom learn the full range of tasks once proper to their trade [Marshall 1972: 42–6].

THE APPRENTICESHIP OF NONDRINKING ALCOHOLICS

The descriptions of apprenticeship in midwifery, tailoring, and quartermastering provide examples of how learning in practice takes place and what it means to move toward full participation in a community of practice. A more detailed view of the fashioning of identity may be found in an analysis of the process of becoming a nondrinking alcoholic through Alcoholics Anonymous. An apprentice alcoholic attends several meetings a week, spending that time in the company of near-peers and adepts, those whose practice and identities are the community of A. A. At these meetings old-timers give testimony about

79

their drinking past and the course of the process of becoming sober. In addition to "general meetings," where old-timers may tell polished, hour-long stories – months and years in the making – of their lives as alcoholics, there are also smaller "discussion meetings," which tend to focus on a single aspect of what in the end will be a part of the reconstructed life story (Cain n.d.).

The notion of partial participation, in segments of work that increase in complexity and scope, a theme in all the analyses of apprenticeship discussed here, also describes the changing form of participation in A. A. for newcomers as they gradually become old-timers. In the testimony at early meetings new-comers have access to a comprehensive view of what the community is about. Goals are also made plain in the litany of the "Twelve Steps" to sobriety, which guide the process of moving from peripheral to full participation in A. A., much as the garment inventory of the tailors' apprentices serves as an itinerary for their progress through apprenticeship. The contribution of an absolutely new member may be no more than one silent gesture – picking up a white chip at the end of the meeting to indicate the intention not to take a drink during the next 24 hours (Cain n.d.). In due course, the Twelfth-Step visit to an active drinker to try to persuade that person to become a newcomer in the organization initiates a new phase of participation, now as a recognized old-timer. Cain (n.d.) argues that the main business of A. A. is the reconstruction of identity, through the process of constructing personal life stories, and with them, the meaning of the teller's past and future action in the world.

The change men and women . . . undergo . . . is much more than a change in behavior. It is a transformation of their identities, from drinking non-alcoholics to nondrinking alcoholics, and it affects how they view and act in the world. . . . One important vehicle for this is the personal story. . . .

By ''identity'' I mean the way a person understands and views himself, and is viewed by others, a perception of self which is fairly constant. . . . There are two important dimensions to the identity of A. A. alcoholic. The first distinction which A. A. makes is alcoholic and non-alcoholic, where alcoholic refers to a state which, once attained, is not reversible. The second is drinking and non-drinking, and refers to a potentially controllable activity. . . . There are therefore two aspects of the A. A. alcoholic identity important for continuing membership in A. A.; qualification as an alcoholic, which is based on one's past, and continued effort at not drinking. The A. A. identity requires a behavior – not drinking – which is a negation of the behavior which originally qualified one for membership. One of the functions of the A. A. personal story is to establish both aspects of membership in an individual. . . . In personal stories, A. A. members tell their own drinking histories, how they came to understand that they are alcoholics, how they got into A. A., and what their life has been like since they joined A. A. . . .

In A. A. personal stories are told for the explicit, stated purpose of providing a model of alcoholism, so that other drinkers may find so much of themselves in the lives of professed alcoholics that they cannot help but ask whether they, too, are alcoholics. Since the definition of an alcoholic is not really agreed on in the wider culture, arriving at this interpretation of events is a process negotiated between the drinker and those around her. A. A. stories provide a set of criteria by which the alcoholic can be identified. . . . A. A. recognizes their importance, and dedicates a significant amount of meeting time and publishing space to the telling of these stories. A. A. members tell personal stories formally in "speakers' meetings." . . . Less formally, members tell shortened versions of their stories, or parts of them, at discussion meetings. . . . The final important context for telling personal stories is in "Twelfth Step calls." When A. A. members talk to outsiders who may be alcoholics in a one-to-one interaction, they are following the last of the Twelve Steps. . . . Ideally, at these individual meetings, the member tells his story, tells about the A. A. program, tries to help the drinker see herself as an alcoholic if she is "ready." [Members] claim that telling their own stories to other alcoholics, and thus helping other alcoholics to achieve sobriety, is an important part of maintaining their own sobriety. [At the same time] telling a personal story, especially at a speaker's meeting or on a Twelfth Step call, signals membership because this "is the time that they [members] feel that they belong enough to 'carry the message'."

Telling an A. A. story is not something one learns through explicit teaching. Newcomers are not told how to tell their stories, yet most people who remain in A. A. learn to do this. There are several ways in which an A. A. member learns to tell an appropriate story. First, he must be exposed to A. A. models. . . . The newcomer to A. A. hears and reads personal stories from the time of early contact with the program –

through meetings, literature, and talk with individual old-timers. . . . In addition to learning from the models, learning takes place through interaction. All members are encouraged to speak at discussions and to maintain friendship with other A. A. members. In the course of this social interaction the new member is called on to talk about her own life. . . . This may be in bits and pieces, rather than the entire life. For example, in discussion meetings, the topic of discussion may be "admitting you are powerless," "making amends," "how to avoid the first drink," or shared experiences in dealing with common problems. . . . One speaker follows another by picking out certain pieces of what has previously been said, saying why it was relevant to him, and elaborating on it with some episode of his own. . . . Usually, unless the interpretation runs counter to A. A. beliefs, the speaker is not corrected. Rather, other speakers will take the appropriate parts of the newcomer's comments, and build on this in their own comments, giving parallel accounts with different interpretations, for example, or expanding on parts of their own stories which are similar to parts of the newcomer's story, while ignoring the inappropriate parts of the newcomer's story.

In addition to the structure of the A. A. story, the newcomers must also learn the cultural model of alcoholism encoded in them, including A. A. propositions, appropriate episodes to serve as evidence, and appropriate interpretations of events. . . . Simply learning the propositions about alcohol and its nature is not enough. They must be applied by the drinker to his own life, and this application must be demonstrated. . . . In A. A. success, or recovery, requires learning to perceive oneself and one's problems from an A. A. perspective. A. A.s must learn to experience their problems as drinking problems, and themselves as alcoholics. Stories do not just describe a life in a learned genre, but are tools for reinterpreting the past, and understanding the self in terms of the A. A. identity. The initiate begins to identify with A. A. members. . . . She comes to understand herself as a non-drinking alcoholic, and to reinterpret her life as evidence.

APPRENTICESHIP AND SITUATED LEARNING: A NEW AGENDA

We have seen apprenticeship here in conjunction with various forms for the organization of production. There are rich relations among community members of all sorts, their activities and artifacts. All are implicated in processes of increasing participation and knowledgeability. To a certain extent the ethnographic studies excerpted here focus on different facets of apprenticeship. The Yucatec study addresses the puzzle of how learning can occur without teaching and without formally organized apprenticeship. The analysis of Vai apprenticeship contributes to resolving the puzzle in laying out the curriculum of everyday practice in Vai tailor shops. Hutchins analyzes relations between the flow of information in a pivotal task and the trajectories of persons through different forms of participation in the task, in the course of which he problematizes the question of learners' access to important learning resources.

Once raised, the "dark side" of questions of access, vividly laid out in the butchers' example, helps to underline the crucial character of broad, and broadly legitimate, peripheral participation in a community of practice as central for increasing understanding and identity. And turned back on the Yucatec and Vai studies, these questions suggest a transmutation of preoccupations with teaching and with formal, intentional learning situations into cases in which access to all the means and grounds of membership is virtually a matter of course. If masters don't teach, they embody practice at its fullest in the community of practice. Becoming a "member such as those" is an embodied telos too complex to be discussed in the narrower and simpler language of goals, tasks, and knowledge acquisition. There may be no language for participants with which to discuss it at all – but identities of mastery, in all their complications, are there to be assumed (in both senses).

The importance of language should not, however, be overlooked. Language is part of practice, and it is in practice that people learn. In Cain's ethnographic study of identity construction in A. A., talk is a central medium of transformation. Whether activity or language is the central issue, the important point concerning learning is one of access to practice as resource for learning, rather than to instruction. Issues of motivation, identity, and language deserve further discussion.

We would be remiss, in any discussion of converging characterizations of apprenticeship, if we did not include Becker's pathbreaking analysis, which preceded all the ethnographic studies discussed here with the exception of Marshall's. Indeed, he compared research in schools with research on American trade apprenticeship, including Marshall's research on the butchers. He insisted on the significance of the broad initial view that taking part in ongoing work activities offers to newcomers, the value of being in relevant settings for learning, the existence of strong goals for learning in work-learning settings, the absence of tests, and the greater effectiveness of apprenticeship than school. He further assumed, in contradistinction to the examples discussed here, that teaching is central to learning through apprenticeship; and that apprentices, individually, must organize their own learning "curriculum" and recruit teaching or guidance for themselves.

In these respects, the present studies pose novel questions, given their more insistent focus on learning resources in the community than on teaching and "pupil initiative." However, they are perhaps too quick to assume that an explanation of community learning resources is to be found in the "work-driven" nature of apprenticeship. If apprenticeship is a form of education in which work and learning are seamlessly related, it is nonetheless a form in which the work and understanding of newcomers bear complex and changing relations with ongoing work processes; the structure of production and the structure of apprenticeship do not coincide as a whole (though they may do so for given tasks, e.g., plot-fixing for the quartermasters). This has interesting, also complex, implications for processes of deepening and changing understanding for all members of a community of practice.

Becker raises a serious new set of concerns about the issue of access. He recognizes the disastrous possibilities that structural constraints in work organizations may curtail or extinguish apprentices' access to the full range of activities of the job, and hence to possibilities for learning what they need to know to master a trade. In particular, he raises more acutely than the ethnographic studies discussed here the conflictual character of access for newcomers, the problems about power and control on which these studies are on the whole silent.

Neither Becker nor the ethnographic studies address the implications of conflictual community practice in conjunction with identity development, a problem to be taken up shortly.

In sum, a first reading of these examples along with Becker's work, takes us a considerable distance in redescribing and resetting an agenda of questions for the analysis of situated learning. But we will need to turn the problems of access, of its embedding in the conflictual forms of everyday practice, of motivation, and of the development of membership/identity into objects of analysis. The theoretical framework of legitimate peripheral participation may be used to launch us on this task in the next chapter.

4

Legitimate Peripheral Participation in Communities of Practice

In Communities of Practice

We now can begin to turn the observations of the previous chapter into objects to be analyzed. In the following sections, we recast the central characteristics of these several historical realizations of apprenticeship in terms of legitimate peripheral participation. First, we discuss the structuring resources that shape the process and content of learning possibilities and apprentices' changing perspectives on what is known and done. Then we argue that "transparency" of the sociopolitical organization of practice, of its content and of the artifacts engaged in practice, is a crucial resource for increasing participation. We next examine the relation of newcomers to the discourse of practice. This leads to a discussion of how identity and motivation are generated as newcomers move toward full participation. Finally, we explore contradictions inherent in learning, and the relations of the resulting conflicts to the development of identity and the transformation of practice.

STRUCTURING RESOURCES FOR LEARNING IN PRACTICE

One of the first things people think of when apprenticeship is mentioned is the master–apprentice relation. But in practice the roles of masters are surprisingly variable across time and place. A specific master–apprentice relation is not even ubiquitously characteristic of apprenticeship learning. Indeed, neither Yucatec midwives nor quartermasters learn in specific master–apprentice relations. Newcomers to A. A. do have special relations with specific old-timers who act as their sponsors, but these relations are not what defines them as newcomers. In contrast, tailors' apprentices most certainly have spe-

91

cific relations with their masters, without whom they wouldn't be apprentices. Master tailors must sponsor apprentices before the latter can have legitimate access to participation in the community's productive activities. In short, the form in which such legitimate access is secured for apprentices depends on the characteristics of the division of labor in the social milieu in which the community of practice is located. Thus, the midwife is learning a specialism within her own family of orientation, a form of labor different, but not separated in marked ways, from the widely distributed "ordinary" activities of everyday life; legitimate participation comes diffusely through membership in family and community. Where apprentices learn a specialized occupation, sponsorship into a community of practice – within a community in the more general sense – becomes an issue. Intentional relations, and even contractual relations with a specific master, are common. It should be clear that, in shaping the relation of masters to apprentices, the issue of conferring legitimacy is more important than the issue of providing teaching.

Even in the case of the tailors, where the relation of apprentice to master is specific and explicit, it is not this relationship, but rather the apprentice's relations to other apprentices and even to other masters that organize opportunities to learn; an apprentice's own master is too distant, an object of too much respect, to engage with in awkward attempts at a new activity. In A. A., old-timers who act as "sponsors" reportedly withhold advice and instruction appropriate to later stages; they hold back and wait until the newcomer becomes "ready" for a next step through increasing participation in the community (Alibrandi 1977). In all five cases described in the preceding chapter, in fact, researchers insist that there is very little observable teaching; the more basic phenomenon is learning. The practice of the community creates the potential "curriculum" in the broadest sense – that which may be learned by newcomers with legitimate peripheral access. Learning activity appears to have a characteristic pattern. There are strong goals for learning because learners, as peripheral participants, can develop a view of what the whole enterprise is about, and what there is to be learned. Learning itself is an improvised practice: A learning curriculum unfolds in opportunities for engagement in practice. It is not specified as a set of dictates for proper practice.

In apprenticeship opportunities for learning are, more often than not, given structure by work practices instead of by strongly asymmetrical master–apprentice relations. Under these circumstances learners may have a space of "benign community neglect" in which to configure their own learning relations with other apprentices. There may be a looser coupling between relations among learner on the one hand and the often hierarchical relations between learners and old-timers on the other hand, than where directive pedagogy is the central motive of institutional organization. It seems typical of apprenticeship that apprentices learn mostly in relation with other apprentices. There is anecdotal evidence (Butler personal communication; Hass n.d.) that where the circulation of knowledge among peers and near-peers is possible, it spreads exceedingly rapidly and effectively. The central grounds on which forms of education that differ from schooling are condemned are that changing the person is not the central motive of the enterprise in which learning takes place (see the last section of this chapter). The effectiveness of the circulation of information among peers suggests, to the contrary, that engaging in practice, rather than being its object, may well be a *condition* for the effectiveness of learning.

So far, we have observed that the authority of masters and their involvement in apprenticeship varies dramatically across communities of practice. We have also pointed out that structuring resources for learning come from a variety of sources, not only from pedagogical activity. We argue that a coherent explanation of these observations depends upon *decentering* common notions of mastery and pedagogy. This decentering strategy is, in fact, deeply embedded in our situated approach – for to shift as we have from the notion of an individual learner to the concept of legitimate peripheral participation in communities of practice is precisely to decenter analysis of learning. To take a decentered view of master–apprentice relations leads to an understanding that mastery resides not in the master but in the organization of the community of practice of which the master is part: The master as the locus of authority (in several senses) is, after all, as much a product of the conventional, centered theory of learning as is the individual learner. Similarly, a decentered view of the master as pedagogue moves the focus of analysis away from teaching and onto the intricate structuring of a community's learning resources.

THE PLACE OF KNOWLEDGE: PARTICIPATION, LEARNING CURRICULA, COMMUNITIES OF PRACTICE

The social relations of apprentices within a community change through their direct involvement in activities; in the process, the apprentices' understanding and knowledgeable skills develop. In the recent past, the only means we have had for understanding the processes by which these changes occur have come from conventional speculations about the nature of "informal" learning: That is, apprentices are supposed to acquire the "specifics" of practice through "observation and imitation." But this view is in all probability wrong in every particular, or right in particular circumstances, but for the wrong reasons. We argue instead that the effects of peripheral participation on knowledge-in-practice are not properly understood; and that studies of apprenticeship have presumed too literal a coupling of work processes and learning processes.

To begin with, newcomers' legitimate peripherality provides them with more than an "observational" lookout post: It crucially involves *participation* as a way of learning – of both absorbing and being absorbed in – the "culture of practice." An extended period of legitimate peripherality provides learners with opportunities to make the culture of practice theirs. From a broadly peripheral perspective, apprentices gradually assemble a general idea of what constitutes the practice of the community. This uneven sketch of the enterprise (available if there is legitimate access) might include who is involved; what they do; what everyday life is like; how masters talk, walk, work, and generally conduct their lives; how people who are not part of the community of practice interact with it; what other learners are doing; and what learners need to learn to become full practitioners. It includes an increasing understanding of how, when, and about what old-timers collaborate, collude, and collide, and what they enjoy, dislike, respect, and admire. In particular, it offers exemplars (which are grounds and motivation for learning activity), including masters, finished products, and more advanced apprentices in the process of becoming full practitioners.

Such a general view, however, is not likely to be frozen in

initial impressions. Viewpoints from which to understand the practice evolve through changing participation in the division of labor, changing relations to ongoing community practices, and changing social relations in the community. This is as true, in different ways, of reformed alcoholics as they socialize with other A. A. members as it is of quartermasters as they move through different aspects of navigation work. And learners have multiply structured relations with ongoing practice in other ways. Apprenticeship learning is not "work-driven" in the way stereotypes of informal learning have suggested; the ordering of learning and of everyday practice do not coincide. Production activity-segments must be learned in different sequences than those in which a production process commonly unfolds, if peripheral, less intense, less complex, less vital tasks are learned before more central aspects of practice.

Consider, for instance, the tailors' apprentices, whose involvement starts with both initial preparations for the tailors' daily labor and finishing details on completed garments. The apprentices progressively move backward through the production process to cutting jobs. (This kind of progression is quite common across cultures and historical periods.) Under these circumstances, the initial "circumferential" perspective absorbed in partial, peripheral, apparently trivial activities – running errands, delivering messages, or accompanying others – takes on new significance: It provides a first approximation to an armature of the structure of the community of practice. Things learned, and various and changing viewpoints, can be arranged and interrelated in ways that gradually transform that skeletal understanding.

When directive teaching in the form of prescriptions about proper practice generates one circumscribed form of participation (in school), preempting participation in ongoing practice as the legitimate source of learning opportunities, the goal of complying with the requirements specified by teaching engenders a practice different from that intended (Bourdieu 1977). In such cases, even though the pedagogical structure of the circumstances of learning has moved away from the principle of legitimate peripheral participation with respect to the target practice, legitimate peripheral participation is still the core of the learning that takes place. This leads us to distinguish between a *learning curriculum* and a *teaching curriculum*. A learning curriculum consists of situated opportunities (thus including exemplars of various sorts often thought of as "goals") for the improvisational development of new practice (Lave 1989). A learning curriculum is a field of learning resources in everyday practice *viewed from the perspective of learners*. A teaching curriculum, by contrast, is constructed for the instruction of newcomers. When a teaching curriculum supplies – and thereby limits – structuring resources for learning, the meaning of what is learned (and control of access to it, both in its peripheral forms and its subsequently more complex and intensified, though possibly more fragmented, forms) is mediated through an instructor's participation, by an external view of what knowing is about. The learning curriculum in didactic situations, then, evolves out of participation in a specific community of practice engendered by pedagogical relations and by a prescriptive view of the target practice as a subject matter, as well as out of the many and various relations that tie participants to their own and to other institutions.

A learning curriculum is essentially situated. It is not something that can be considered in isolation, manipulated in arbitrary didactic terms, or analyzed apart from the social relations that shape legitimate peripheral participation. A learning curriculum is thus characteristic of a community. In using the

97

term community, we do not imply some primordial culture-sharing entity. We assume that members have different interests, make diverse contributions to activity, and hold varied viewpoints. In our view, participation at multiple levels is entailed in membership in a *community of practice*. Nor does the term community imply necessarily co-presence, a well-defined, identifiable group, or socially visible boundaries. It does imply participation in an activity system about which participants share understandings concerning what they are doing and what that means in their lives and for their communities.

The concept of community underlying the notion of legitimate peripheral participation, and hence of "knowledge" and its "location" in the lived-in world, is both crucial and subtle. The community of practice of midwifery or tailoring involves much more than the technical knowledgeable skill involved in delivering babies or producing clothes. A community of practice is a set of relations among persons, activity, and world, over time and in relation with other tangential and overlapping communities of practice. A community of practice is an intrinsic condition for the existence of knowledge, not least because it provides the interpretive support necessary for making sense of its heritage. Thus, participation in the cultural practice in which any knowledge exists is an epistemological principle of learning. The social structure of this practice, its power relations, and its conditions for legitimacy define possibilities for learning (i.e., for legitimate peripheral participation).

It is possible to delineate the community that is the site of a learning process by analyzing the reproduction cycles of the communities that seem to be involved and their relations. For the quartermasters, the cycle of navigational practice is quite short; a complete reproduction of the practice of quartermastering may take place every five or six years (as a novice enters, gradually becomes a full participant, begins to work with newcomer quartermasters who in their own turn become full participants and reach the point at which they are ready to work with newcomers). The reproduction cycle of the midwives', the tailors', or the butchers' communities is much longer. In A. A., its length is rather variable as individuals go through successive steps at their own pace. Observing the span of developmental cycles is only a beginning to such an analysis (and a rough approximation that sets aside consideration of the transformation and change inherent in ongoing practice – see below), for each such cycle has its own trajectory, benchmarks, blueprints, and careers (Stack 1989).

In addition to the useful analytic questions suggested by a temporal focus on communities of practice, there is a further reason to address the delineation of communities of practice in processual, historical terms. Claims *about* the definition of a community of practice and the community of practice actually in process of reproduction in that location may not coincide – a point worth careful consideration.

For example, in most high schools there is a group of students engaged over a substantial period of time in learning physics. What community of practice is in the process of reproduction? Possibly the students participate only in the reproduction of the high school itself. But assuming that the practice of physics is also being reproduced in some form, there are vast differences between the ways high school physics students participate in and give meaning to their activity and the way professional physicists do. The actual reproducing community of practice, within which schoolchildren learn about physics, is not the community of physicists but the community of schooled adults. Children are introduced into the latter community (and its humble relation with the former community) during their school years. The reproduction cycles of the physicists' community start much later, possibly only in graduate school (Traweek 1988).

In this view, problems of schooling are not, at their most fundamental level, pedagogical. Above all, they have to do with the ways in which the community of adults reproduces itself, with the places that newcomers can or cannot find in such communities, and with relations that can or cannot be established between these newcomers and the cultural and political life of the community.

In summary, rather than learning by replicating the performances of others or by acquiring knowledge transmitted in instruction, we suggest that learning occurs through centripetal participation in the learning curriculum of the ambient community. Because the place of knowledge is within a community of practice, questions of learning must be addressed within the developmental cycles of that community, a recommendation which creates a diagnostic tool for distinguishing among communities of practice.

THE PROBLEM OF ACCESS: TRANSPARENCY AND
SEQUESTRATION

The key to legitimate peripherality is access by newcomers to the community of practice and all that membership entails. But though this is essential to the reproduction of any community, it is always problematic at the same time. To become a full member of a community of practice requires access to a wide range of ongoing activity, old-timers, and other members of the community; and to information, resources, and opportunities for participation. The issue is so central to membership in communities of practice that, in a sense, all that we have said so far is about access. Here we discuss the problem more specifically in connection with issues of understanding and control, which along with involvement in productive activity are related aspects of the legitimate peripherality of participants in a practice.

The artifacts employed in ongoing practice, the technology of practice, provide a good arena in which to discuss the problem of access to understanding. In general, social scientists who concern themselves with learning treat technology as a given and are not analytic about its interrelations with other aspects of a community of practice. Becoming a full participant certainly includes engaging with the technologies of everyday practice, as well as participating in the social relations, production processes, and other activities of communities of practice. But the understanding to be gained from engagement with technology can be extremely varied depending on the form of participation enabled by its use. Participation involving technology is especially significant because the artifacts used within a cultural practice carry a substantial portion of that practice's heritage. For example, the alidade used by the quartermasters for taking bearings has developed as a navigational instrument over hundreds of years, and embodies calculations invented long ago (Hutchins in press). Thus, understanding the technology of practice is more than learning to use tools; it is a way to connect with the history of the practice and to participate more directly in its cultural life.

The significance of artifacts in the full complexity of their relations with the practice can be more or less *transparent* to learners. Transparency in its simplest form may just imply that the inner workings of an artifact are available for the learner's inspection: The black box can be opened, it can become a "glass box." But there is more to understanding the use and significance of an artifact: Knowledge within a community of practice and ways of perceiving and manipulating objects characteristic of community practices are encoded in artifacts in ways that can be more or less revealing. Moreover, the activity system and the social world of which an artifact is part are reflected in multiple ways in its design and use and can become further "fields of transparency," just as they can remain opaque. Obviously, the transparency of any technology always exists with respect to some purpose and is intricately tied to the cultural practice and social organization within which the technology is meant to function: It cannot be viewed as a feature of an artifact in itself but as a process that involves specific forms of participation, in which the technology fulfills a mediating function. Apprentice quartermasters not only have access to the physical activities going on around them and to the tools of the trade; they participate in information flows and conversations, in a context in which they can make sense of what they observe and hear. In focusing on the epistemological role of artifacts in the context of the social organization of knowledge, this notion of transparency constitutes, as it were, the cultural organization of access. As such, it does not apply to technology only, but to all forms of access to practice.

Productive activity and understanding are not separate, or even separable, but dialectically related. Thus, the term *transparency* when used here in connection with technology refers to the way in which using artifacts and understanding their significance interact to become one learning process. Mirroring the intricate relation between using and understanding artifacts, there is an interesting duality inherent in the concept of transparency. It combines the two characteristics of *invisibility* and *visibility*: invisibility in the form of unproblematic interpretation and integration into activity, and visibility in the form of extended access to information. This is not a simple dichotomous distinction, since these two crucial characteristics are in a complex interplay, their relation being one of both conflict and synergy.

It might be useful to give a sense of this interplay by analogy to a window. A window's invisibility is what makes it a window, that is, an object through which the world outside becomes visible. The very fact, however, that so many things can be seen through it makes the window itself highly visible, that is, very salient in a room, when compared to, say, a solid wall. Invisibility of mediating technologies is necessary for allowing focus on, and thus supporting visibility of, the subject matter. Conversely, visibility of the significance of the technology is necessary for allowing its unproblematic – invisible – use. This interplay of conflict and synergy is central to all aspects of learning in practice: It makes the design of supportive artifacts a matter of providing a good balance between these two interacting requirements. (An extended analysis of the concept of transparency can be found in Wenger 1990.)

Control and selection, as well as the need for access, are inherent in communities of practice. Thus access is liable to manipulation, giving legitimate peripherality an ambivalent status: Depending on the organization of access, legitimate peripherality can either promote or prevent legitimate participation. In the study of the butchers' apprentices, Marshall provides examples of how access can be denied. The trade school and its shop exercises did not simulate the central practices of meat cutting in supermarkets, much less make them accessible to apprentices; on-the-job training was not much of an improvement. Worse, the master butchers confined their apprentices to jobs that were removed from activities rather than peripheral to them. To the extent that the community of practice routinely sequesters newcomers, either very directly as in the example of apprenticeship for the butchers, or in more subtle and pervasive ways as in schools, these newcomers are prevented from peripheral participation. In either case legitimacy is not in question. Schoolchildren are legitimately peripheral, but kept from participation in the social world more generally. The butchers' apprentices participate legitimately, but not peripherally, in that they are not given productive access to activity in the community of practitioners.

An important point about such sequestering when it is institutionalized is that it encourages a folk epistemology of dichotomies, for instance, between "abstract" and "concrete" knowledge. These categories do not reside in the world as distinct forms of *knowledge,* nor do they reflect some putative hierarchy of forms of knowledge among practitioners. Rather, they derive from the nature of the new practice generated by sequestration. *Abstraction* in this sense stems from the disconnectedness of a particular cultural practice. Participation in that practice is neither more nor less abstract or concrete, experiential or cerebral, than in any other. Thus, legitimate peripheral participation as the core concept of relations of learning places the explanatory burden for issues such as "understanding" and "levels" of abstraction or conceptualization not on one type of learning as opposed to another, but on the cultural practice in which the learning is taking place, on issues of access, and on the transparency of the cultural environment with respect to the meaning of what is being learned. Insofar as the notion of transparency, taken very broadly, is a way of organizing activities that makes their meaning visible, it opens an alternative approach to the traditional dichotomy between learning experientially and learning at a distance, between learning by doing and learning by abstraction.

DISCOURSE AND PRACTICE

The characterization of language in learning has, in discussions of conventional contrasts between formal and informal learning, been treated as highly significant in classifying ways of transmitting knowledge. Verbal instruction has been assumed to have special, and especially effective properties with respect to the generality and scope of the understanding that learners come away with, while instruction by demonstration – learning by "observation and imitation" – is supposed to produce the opposite, a literal and narrow effect.

Close analysis of both instructional discourse and cases of apprenticeship raise a different point: Issues about language, like those about the role of masters, may well have more to do with legitimacy of participation and with access to peripherality than they do with knowledge transmission. Indeed, as Jordan (1989) argues, learning to become a legitimate participant in a community involves learning how to talk (and be silent) in the manner of full participants. In A. A. telling the story of the life of the nondrinking alcoholic is clearly a major vehicle for the display of membership. Models for constructing A. A. life stories are widely available in published accounts of alco-

105

holics' lives and in the storytelling performances of old-timers. Early on, newcomers learn to preface their contributions to A.A. meetings with the simple identifying statement "I'm a recovering alcoholic," and, shortly, to introduce themselves and sketch the problems that brought them to A.A. They begin by describing these events in non–A.A. terms. Their accounts meet with counterexemplary stories by more-experienced members who do not criticize or correct newcomers' accounts directly. They gradually generate a view that matches more closely the A.A. model, eventually producing skilled testimony in public meetings and gaining validation from others as they demonstrate the appropriate understanding.

The process of learning to speak as a full member of a community of practice is vividly illustrated in an analysis of the changing performances of newcomer spirit mediums in a spiritist congregation in Mexico (Kearney 1977). This example is interesting partly because the notion of "proper speech" is so clearly crystallized in the collective expectations of the community, while at the same time, if the community were forced to acknowledge the idea that mediums must *learn* their craft, this would negate the legitimacy of spirit possession. That learning through legitimate peripheral participation nonetheless occurs makes this example especially striking.

Spiritist cult communities center around women who are adept at going into trance. They act as mediums, transmitting the messages of a variety of spirits. The spirits are arranged in a complex hierarchy of more- and less-important forms of deity. It takes a great deal of practice to speak coherently while in trance, especially while taking on a variety of personae.

It is quite apparent from biographical data I have on mediums that they typically begin "working" with

106

various [unimportant] exotic spirits who have idiosyn-
cratic speech patterns, and then eventually switch to
working with the [highly revered] Divinities who typically speak in a much more stereotypic manner. . . .
Recently several novice mediums have been "entered"
by "beings from outer space." These beings appeared
quite intent on speaking to those present via the mediums, but of course their language was incomprehen-
sible to the audience. During the course of repeated
visits, however, and with help from nonpossessed
spiritualists, they slowly "began to learn to speak the
Spanish language," and to articulate their messages.
. . . A . . . characteristic of advanced mediums as
compared with novices is the large repertoire and wider
range of identities displayed by the former [Kearney
1977].

In the *Psychology of Literacy,* Scribner and Cole (1981) spec-
ulate that asking questions – learning how to "do" school
appropriately – may be a major part of what school teaches.
This is also Jordan's conclusion about Yucatec midwives' participation in biomedical, state-sponsored training courses. She
argues that the verbal instruction provided by health officials
has the effect of teaching midwives how to talk in biomedical
terms when required. Such talk only serves to give them "face
validity" in the eyes of others who believe in the authoritative
character of biomedicine. But Jordan argues that it has no effect on their existing practice.

This point about language use is consonant with the earlier
argument that didactic instruction creates unintended practices. The conflict stems from the fact that there is a difference
between talking *about* a practice from outside and talking *within*

it. Thus the didactic use of language, not itself the discourse of practice, creates a new linguistic practice, which has an existence of its own. Legitimate peripheral participation in such linguistic practice is a form of learning, but does not imply that newcomers learn the actual practice the language is supposed to be about.

In a community or practice, there are no special forms of discourse aimed at apprentices or crucial to their centripetal movement toward full participation that correspond to the marked genres of the question–answer–evaluation format of classroom teaching, or the lecturing of college professors or midwife-training course instructors. But Jordan makes a further, acute, observation about language, this time about the role of *stories* in apprenticeship: She points out that stories play a major role in decision making (1989). This has implications for what and how newcomers learn. For apprenticeship learning is supported by conversations and stories about problematic and especially difficult cases.

> What happens is that as difficulties of one kind or another develop, stories of similar cases are offered up by the attendants [at a birth], all of whom, it should be remembered, are experts, having themselves given birth. In the ways in which these stories are treated, elaborated, ignored, taken up, characterized as typical and so on, the collaborative work of deciding on the present case is done. . . . These stories, then, are packages of situated knowledge. . . . To acquire a store of appropriate stories and, even more importantly, to know what are appropriate occasions for telling them, is then part of what it means to become a midwife [1989: 935].

108

In Communities of Practice

Orr (in press) describes comparable patterns of story telling in his research on the learning of machine-repair work: Technicians who repair copier machines tell each other "war stories" about their past experiences in making repairs. Such stories constitute a vital part of diagnosing and carrying out new repairs. In the process, newcomers learn how to make (sometimes difficult) repairs, they learn the skills of war-story telling, and they become legitimate participants in the community of practice. In A. A. also, discussions have a dual purpose. Participants engage in the work of staying sober and they do so through gradual construction of an identity. Telling the personal story is a tool of diagnosis and reinterpretation. Its communal use is essential to the fashioning of an identity as a recovered alcoholic, and thus to remaining sober. It becomes a display of membership by virtue of fulfilling a crucial function in the shared practice.

It is thus necessary to refine our distinction between *talking about* and *talking within* a practice. Talking within itself includes both talking within (e.g., exchanging information necessary to the progress of ongoing activities) and talking about (e.g., stories, community lore). Inside the shared practice, both forms of talk fulfill specific functions: engaging, focusing, and shifting attention, bringing about coordination, etc., on the one hand; and supporting communal forms of memory and reflection, as well as signaling membership, on the other. (And, similarly, talking about includes both forms of talk once it becomes part of a practice of its own, usually sequestered in some respects.) For newcomers then the purpose is not to learn *from* talk as a substitute for legitimate peripheral participation; it is to learn *to* talk as a key to legitimate peripheral participation.

109

Situated Learning

MOTIVATION AND IDENTITY: EFFECTS OF PARTICIPATION

It is important to emphasize that, during the extended period of legitimate participation typical of the cases of apprenticeship described here, newcomers participate in a community of practitioners as well as in productive activity. Legitimate peripheral participation is an initial form of membership characteristic of such a community. Acceptance by and interaction with acknowledged adept practitioners make learning legitimate and of value from the point of view of the apprentice. More generally, learning in practice, apprentice learners know that there is a field for the mature practice of what they are learning to do – midwifing, tailoring, quartermastering, butchering, or being sober. The community of midwives, tailors, quartermasters, butchers, or nondrinking alcoholics and their productive relations with the world provide apprentices with these continuity-based "futures."

To be able to participate in a legitimately peripheral way entails that newcomers have broad access to arenas of mature practice. At the same time, productive peripherality requires less demands on time, effort, and responsibility for work than for full participants. A newcomer's tasks are short and simple, the costs of errors are small, the apprentice has little responsibility for the activity as a whole. A newcomer's tasks tend to be positioned at the ends of branches of work processes, rather than in the middle of linked work segments. A midwife's apprentice runs errands. Tailors' apprentices do maintenance on the sewing machine before the master begins work, and finishing details when the master has completed a pair of trousers; a lot of time in between is spent sitting beside the master on his

110

two-person bench. For the quartermasters, the earliest jobs are physically at the periphery of the work space. In many cases, distinctions between play and work, or between peripheral activity and other work, are little marked. In all five cases of apprenticeship, however, it is also true that the initial, partial contributions of apprentices are useful. Even the A. A. newcomer, while reinterpreting his or her life, produces new material that contributes to the communal construction of an understanding of alcoholism. An apprentice's contributions to ongoing activity gain value in practice – a value which increases as the apprentice becomes more adept. As opportunities for understanding how well or poorly one's efforts contribute are evident in practice, legitimate participation of a peripheral kind provides an immediate ground for self-evaluation. The sparsity of tests, praise, or blame typical of apprenticeship follows from the apprentice's legitimacy as a participant.

Notions like those of "intrinsic rewards" in empirical studies of apprenticeship focus quite narrowly on task knowledge and skill as the activities to be learned. Such knowledge is of course important; but a deeper sense of the value of participation to the community and the learner lies in *becoming* part of the community. Thus, making a hat reasonably well is seen as evidence that an apprentice tailor is becoming "a masterful practitioner," though it may also be perceived in a more utilitarian vein in terms of reward or even value. Similarly, telling one's life story or making a Twelfth Step call confers a sense of belonging. Moving toward full participation in practice involves not just a greater commitment of time, intensified effort, more and broader responsibilities within the community, and more difficult and risky tasks, but, more significantly, an increasing sense of identity as a master practitioner.

Situated Learning

When the process of increasing participation is not the primary motivation for learning, it is often because "didactic caretakers" assume responsibility for motivating newcomers. In such circumstances, the focus of attention shifts from co-participating in practice to acting upon the person-to-be-changed. Such a shift is typical of situations, such as schooling, in which pedagogically structured content organizes learning activities. Overlooking the importance of legitimate participation by newcomers in the target practice has two related consequences. First, the identity of learners becomes an explicit object of change. When central participation is the subjective intention motivating learning, changes in cultural identity and social relations are inevitably part of the process, but learning does not have to be mediated – and distorted – through a learner's view of "self" as *object*. Second, where there is no cultural identity encompassing the activity in which newcomers participate and no field of mature practice for what is being learned, exchange value replaces the use value of increasing participation. The commoditization of learning engenders a fundamental contradiction between the use and exchange values of the outcome of learning, which manifests itself in conflicts between learning to know and learning to display knowledge for evaluation. Testing in schools and trade schools (unnecessary in situations of apprenticeship learning) is perhaps the most pervasive and salient example of a way of establishing the exchange value of knowledge. Test taking then becomes a new parasitic practice, the goal of which is to increase the exchange value of learning independently of it use value.

In Communities of Practice

CONTRADICTIONS AND CHANGE: CONTINUITY AND DISPLACEMENT

To account for the complexity of participation in social practice, it is essential to give learning and teaching independent status as analytic concepts. Primary reliance on the concept of pedagogical structuring in learning research may well prevent speculation about what teaching consists of, how it is perceived, and how – as perceived – it affects learning. Most analyses of schooling assume, whether intentionally or not, the uniform motivation of teacher and pupils, because they assume, sometimes quite explicitly, that teacher and pupils share the goal of the main activity (e.g., Davydov and Markova 1983). In our view, this assumption has several consequences. First, it ignores the conflicting viewpoints associated with teaching and learning, respectively, and obscures the distortions that ensue (Fajans and Turner in preparation). Furthermore, it reflects too narrowly rationalistic a perspective on the person and motivation. The multiple viewpoints that are characteristic of participation in a community of practice, and thus of legitimate peripheral participation, are to be found in more complex theories of the person-in-society, such as those proposed by critical psychologists. Finally, assumptions of uniformity make it difficult to explore the mechanisms by which processes of change and transformation in communities practice and processes of learning are intricately implicated in each other.

In considering learning as part of social practice, we have focused our attention on the structure of social practice rather than privileging the structure of pedagogy as the source of learning. Learning understood as legitimate peripheral participation is not necessarily or directly dependent on pedagogical goals or official agenda, even in situations in which these goals appear to be a central factor (e.g., classroom instruction, tutoring). We have insisted that exposure to resources for learning is not restricted to a teaching curriculum and that instructional assistance is not construed as a purely interpersonal phenomenon; rather we have argued that learning must be understood with respect to a practice as a whole, with its multiplicity of relations – both within the community and with the world at large. Dissociating learning from pedagogical intentions opens the possibility of mismatch or conflict among practitioners' viewpoints in situations where learning is going on. These differences often must become constitutive of the content of learning.

We mentioned earlier that a major contradiction lies between legitimate peripheral participation as the means of achieving continuity over generations for the community of practice, and the displacement inherent in that same process as full participants are replaced (directly or indirectly) by newcomers-become-old-timers. Both Fortes (1938) and Goody (1989) have commented on this conflict between continuity and displacement, which is surely part of all learning. This tension is in fact fundamental – a basic contradiction of social reproduction, transformation, and change. In recent accounts of learning by activity theorists (e.g., Engeström 1987), the major contradiction underlying the historical development of learning is that of the commodity. Certainly this is fundamental to the historical shaping of social reproduction as well as production. But we believe that a second contradiction – that between continuity and displacement – is also fundamental to the social relations of production and to the social reproduction of labor. Studies of learning might benefit from examining the field of relations generated by these interrelated contradictions. For if production and the social reproduction of persons are mutually entailed in the reproduction of the social order, the contradictions inherent in reproducing persons within the domestic group and other communities of practice do not go away when the form of production changes, but go through transformations of their own. How to characterize these contradictions in changing forms of production is surely the central question underlying a historical understanding of forms of learning, family, and of course, schooling.

The continuity–displacement contradiction is present during apprenticeship, whether apprentice and master jointly have a stake in the increasingly knowledgeable skill of the apprentice, as among the tailors and midwives, or whether there is a conflict between the master's desire for labor and the apprentice's desire to learn (see Goody 1982), as among the meat cutters. The different ways in which old-timers and newcomers establish and maintain identities conflict and generate competing viewpoints on the practice and its development. Newcomers are caught in a dilemma. On the one hand, they need to engage in the existing practice, which has developed over time: to understand it, to participate in it, and to become full members of the community in which it exists. On the other hand, they have a stake in its development as they begin to establish their own identity in its future.

We have claimed that the development of identity is central to the careers of newcomers in communities of practice, and thus fundamental to the concept of legitimate peripheral participation. This is illustrated most vividly by the experience of newcomers to A. A., but we think that it is true of all learning. In fact, we have argued that, from the perspective we have developed here, learning and a sense of identity are inseparable: They are aspects of the same phenomenon.

Insofar as the conflicts in which the continuity–displace-

ment contradiction is manifested involve power – as they do
to a large extent – the way the contradiction is played out
changes as power relations change. Conflicts between masters
and apprentices (or, less individualistically, between generations) take place in the course of everyday participation. Shared
participation is the stage on which the old and the new, the
known and the unknown, the established and the hopeful, act
out their differences and discover their commonalities, mani-
fest their fear of one another, and come to terms with their
need for one another. Each threatens the fulfillment of the other's destiny, just as it is essential to it. Conflict is experienced
and worked out through a shared everyday practice in which
differing viewpoints and common stakes are in interplay.
Learners can be overwhelmed, overawed, and overworked. Yet
even when submissive imitation is the result, learning is never
simply a matter of the "transmission" of knowledge or the
"acquisition" of skill; identity in relation with practice, and
hence knowledge and skill and their significance to the subject
and the community, are never unproblematic. This helps to
account for the common observation that knowers come in a
range of types, from clones to heretics.

Granting legitimate participation to newcomers with their
own viewpoints introduces into any community of practice all
the tensions of the continuity–displacement contradiction. These
may be muted, though not extinguished, by the differences of
power between old-timers and newcomers. As a way in which
the related conflicts are played out in practice, legitimate peripheral participation is far more than just a process of learning
on the part of newcomers. It is a reciprocal relation between
persons and practice. This means that the move of learners
toward full participation in a community of practice does not
take place in a static context. The practice itself is in motion.

Since activity and the participation of individuals involved in it, their knowledge, and their perspectives are mutually constitutive, change is a fundamental property of communities of practice and their activities. Goody (1989) argues that the introduction of strangers into what was previously strictly domestic production (a change that occurred within an expanding market in West Africa in the recent past) led masters to think more comprehensively about the organization of their production activities. She points out that the resulting division of work processes into segments to be learned has been mirrored in subsequent generations in new, increasingly specialized occupations. Legitimate peripherality is important for developing "constructively naive" perspectives or questions. From this point of view, inexperience is an asset to be exploited. It is of use, however, only in the context of participation, when supported by experienced practitioners who both understand its limitations and value its role. Legitimacy of participation is crucial both for this naive involvement to invite reflection on ongoing activity and for the newcomer's occasional contributions to be taken into account. Insofar as this continual interaction of new perspectives is sanctioned, everyone's participation is legitimately peripheral in some respect. In other words, everyone can to some degree be considered a "newcomer" to the future of a changing community.

5

Conclusion

Conclusion

Until recently, the notion of a concept was viewed as something for which clarity, precision, simplicity, and maximum definition seemed commendable. We have tried, in reflective consonance with our theoretical perspective, to reconceive it in interconnected, relational terms. Thus the concept of legitimate peripheral participation obtains its meaning, not in a concise definition of its boundaries, but in its multiple, theoretically generative interconnections with persons, activities, knowing, and world. Exploring these interconnections in specific cases has provided a way to engage in the practice–theory project that insists on participation in the lived-in world as a key unit of analysis in a theory of social practice (which includes learning), and to develop our thinking in the spirit of this theoretically integrative enterprise.

There has crept into our analysis, as we have moved away from conventional notions of learning, an expanded scale of time and a more encompassing view of what constitutes learning activity. Legitimate peripheral participation has led us to emphasize the sustained character of developmental cycles of communities of practice, the gradual process of fashioning relations of identity as a full practitioner, and the enduring strains inherent in the continuity–displacement contradiction. This longer and broader conception of what it means to learn, implied by the concept of legitimate peripheral participation, comes closer to embracing the rich significance of learning in human experience.

We have thus situated learning in the trajectories of participation in which it takes on meaning. These trajectories must themselves be situated in the social world. Theories of practice growing out of psychological orientations – even those focused on activity – have left as an important set of unexplored terms the interconnections of activity and activity systems, and

121

of activity systems and communities, culture, and political economy. We are, then, trying to furnish the social world in a way that begins to do justice to the structured forms and relations in which legitimate peripheral participation takes place. Relational, historical conceptions have emerged from this exercise, and this decentering tendency is characteristic of the means we have explored for grasping "person," "activity," "knowing," and the "social world."

The *person* has been correspondingly transformed into a practitioner, a newcomer becoming an old-timer, whose changing knowledge, skill, and discourse are part of a developing identity – in short, a member of a community of practice. This idea of identity/membership is strongly tied to a conception of motivation. If the person is both member of a community and agent of activity, the concept of the person closely links meaning and action in the world.

Situated learning activity has been transformed into legitimate peripheral participation in communities of practice. Legitimate peripheral participation moves in a centripetal direction, motivated by its location in a field of mature practice. It is motivated by the growing use value of participation, and by newcomers' desires to become full practitioners. Communities of practice have histories and developmental cycles, and reproduce themselves in such a way that the transformation of newcomers into old-timers becomes unremarkably integral to the practice.

Knowing is inherent in the growth and transformation of identities and it is located in relations among practitioners, their practice, the artifacts of that practice, and the social organization and political economy of communities of practice. For newcomers, their shifting location as they move centripetally through a complex form of practice creates possibilities for

122

understanding the world as experienced. Denying access and limiting the centripetal movement of newcomers and other practitioners changes the learning curriculum. This raises questions – in specific settings, we hope – about what opportunities exist for knowing in practice: about the process of transparency for newcomers. These questions remain distinct from either official or idealized versions of what is meant to be learned or should be learnable.

All of this takes place in a *social world,* dialetically constituted in social practices that are in the process of reproduction, transformation, and change. The challenging problem has been to address the structural character of that world at the level at which it is lived. As a conceptual bridge, legitimate peripheral participation has allowed us to generate analytic terms and questions fundamental to this analysis. In addition to forms of membership and construction of identities, these terms and questions include the location and organization of mastery in communities; problems of power, access, and transparency; developmental cycles of communities of practice; change as part of what it means to be a community of practice; and its basis in the contradiction between continuity and displacement.

References

Alibrandi, L. A. 1977. The recovery process in Alcoholics Anonymous: The sponsor as folk therapist. Social Sciences Working Paper 130. University of California, Irvine.

Bakhurst, D. 1988. Activity, consciousness, and communication. Philosophy Department Report. Oxford University, Oxford.

Bauman, Z. 1973. *Culture as praxis*. London: Routledge and Kegan Paul.

Becker, H. 1972. A school is a lousy place to learn anything in. *American Behavioral Scientist* 16: 85–105.

Bourdieu, P. 1977. *Outline of a theory of practice*. Cambridge: Cambridge University Press.

Cain, Carol. In preparation. Becoming a non-drinking alcoholic: A case study in identity acquisition. Anthropology Department. University of North Carolina, Chapel Hill.

Cooper, E. 1980. *The wood carvers of Hong Kong: Craft production in the world capitalist periphery*. Cambridge: Cambridge University Press.

Coy, M. 1989. *Anthropological perspectives on apprenticeship*. New York: SUNY Press.

Davydov, V. and A. Markova. 1983. A concept of educational activity for school children. *Soviet Psychology* 11(2): 50–76.

Dreier, O. In press. Re-searching psychotherapeutic practice, in S.

References

Chaiklin and J. Lave (eds.), *Understanding practice*. New York: Cambridge University Press.

Engeström, Y. 1987. *Learning by expanding*. Helsinki: Orienta-Konsultit Oy.

Fajans, J. and T. Turner. In preparation. Where the action is: An anthropological perspective on "activity theory," with ethnographic applications. Paper presented at the annual meeting of the American Anthropolitical Association, 1988.

Fortes, M. 1938. Social and psychological aspects of education in Taleland. (Supplement to *Africa* 11(4)).

Garner, J. 1986. *The political dimension of critical psychology*. Berlin: Psychology Institute, Free University of Berlin.

Geer, B. (ed.). 1972. *Learning to work*. Beverly Hills, CA: Sage Publications.

Giddens, A. 1979. *Central problems in social theory: Action, structure, and contradiction in social analysis*. Berkeley: University of California Press.

Goody, E. (ed.). 1982. *From craft to industry*. Cambridge: Cambridge University Press.

1989. Learning and the division of labor, in M. Coy (ed.), *Anthropological perspectives on apprenticeship*. New York: SUNY Press.

Greenfield, P. 1984. A theory of the teacher in the learning activities of everyday life, in B. Rogoff and J. Lave (eds.), *Everyday cognition: Its development in social context*. Cambridge, MA: Harvard University Press.

Griffin, P. and M. Cole. 1984. Current activity for the future: The ZOPED, in B. Rogoff and J. Wertsch (eds.), *Children's learning in the zone of proximal development*. San Francisco: Jossey Bass.

Grosshans, R. R. 1989. Apprenticeship and youth employment: The formation and persistence of an ideology. Paper presented at the annual meeting of the American Educational Research Association. San Francisco, CA, March 1989.

126

References

Haas, J. 1972. Binging: Educational control among high steel iron-workers, in Geer, B. (ed.), *Learning to work*. Beverly Hills, CA: Sage Publications.

Hall, S. 1973. A "reading" of Marx's 1857 "Introduction to the Grundrisse." General Series: Stencilled Occasional Paper No. 1. Center for Contemporary Cultural Studies. University of Birmingham, U.K.

Hanks, William F. 1990. *Referential practice, language, and lived space among the Maya*. Chicago: University of Chicago Press.

Hass, M. n.d. Cognition-in-context: The social nature of the transformation of mathematical knowledge in a third-grade classroom. Program in Social Relations, University of California, Irvine.

Hedegaard, M. 1988. *The zone of proximal development as a basis for instruction*. Aarhus, Denmark: Institute of Psychology.

Holzkamp, K. 1983. *Grundlegung der Psychologie*. Frankfurt/Main: Campus.

1987. Critical psychology and overcoming of scientific indeterminacy in psychological theorizing (L. Zusne, trans.), in R. Hogan and W. H. Jones (eds.), *Perspectives in personality*. Greenwich, CT: JAI Press.

Hutchins, E. In press. Learning to navigate, in S. Chaiklin and J. Lave (eds.), *Understanding practice*. New York: Cambridge University Press.

Ilyenkov, E. V. 1977. *Dialectical logic: Essays on its history and theory*. Moscow: Progress Publishers.

Jordan, B. 1989. Cosmopolitical obstetrics: Some insights from the training of traditional midwives. *Social Science and Medicine* 28(9): 925–44.

Kearney, M. 1977. Oral performance by Mexican spiritualists in possession trance. *Journal of Latin American Lore* 3(2): 309–28.

Lave, J. 1988. *Cognition in practice: Mind, mathematics, and cul-*

References

ture in everyday life. Cambridge: Cambridge University Press.

1989. The acquisition of culture and the practice of understanding, in J. Stigler, R. Shweder, and G. Herdt (eds.), *The Chicago symposia on human development*. Cambridge: Cambridge University Press.

In preparation. *Tailored learning: Apprenticeship and everyday practice among craftsmen in West Africa*.

Marshall, H. 1972. Structural constraints on learning, in B. Geer (ed.), *Learning to work*. Beverly Hills, CA: Sage Publications.

Marx, K. 1857. Introduction to a critique of political economy. Version of the introduction to the *Grundrisse* published as supplementary text in C. J. Arthur (ed.), *The German ideology*, 1988. New York: International Publishers.

Medick, H. 1976. The proto-industrial family economy: The structural function of household and family during the transition from peasant society to industrial capitalism. *Social History* 3: 289–315.

Orr, J. 1986. Narratives at work: Story telling as cooperative diagnostic activity. Proceedings of the Conference on Computer Supported Cooperative Work. Austin, Texas.

In press. Sharing knowledge, celebrating identity: War stories and community memory among service technicians, in D. S. Middleton and D. Edwards (eds.), *Collective remembering: Memory in society*. Beverly Hills, CA: Sage Publications.

Ortner, S. B. 1984. Theory in anthropology since the sixties. *Comparative Studies in Society and History* 26(1): 126–66.

Scribner, S. and M. Cole. 1981. *The psychology of literacy*. Cambridge, MA: Harvard University Press.

Stack, C. 1989. Life trajectories and ethnography. Proposal to the Group on Lifespan Research. University of California, Berkeley.

Traweek, S. 1988. Discovering machines: Nature in the age of its

References

mechanical reproduction, in F. Dubinskas (ed.), *Making time: Ethnographies of high technology organizations*. Philadelphia: Temple University Press.

Wenger, E. 1990. Toward a theory of cultural transparency: elements of a social discourse of the visible and the invisible. Palo Alto, CA: Institute for Research on Learning.

Wertsch, J. (ed.) 1981. *The concept of activity in Soviet psychology*. Armonk, NY: Sharpe.

Wertsch, J. (ed.) 1985. *Culture, communication, and cognition: Vygotskian perspectives*. New York: Cambridge University Press.

Wood, D., J. Bruner, and G. Ross. 1976. The role of tutoring in problem solving. *Journal of Child Psychology and Psychiatry* 17: 89–100.

Index

131

Index

certificate, 67, 77 (*see also* formal versus informal)
change, 57, **113–14,** 123 (*see also* improvisation; reproduction; transformation)
children, 19, 32, 54, 68–9, 70, 99–100, 104
China, 63
circulation, *see* information, flow of
classroom instruction, *see* schooling; teaching
clones, 116
code, 16, 21
cognitive apprenticeship, 29
cognitive processes, 14, 34, 43, 50, 52 (*see also* individualistic perspectives)
cognitive research, 15, 31, 61 (*see also* conventional theories)
Cole, M., 48, 107
collaborative work, 73, 108
collectivist interpretation, 49
commoditization, 114
    of labor, 76
    of learning, 112
communication, 14, 16, 51, 75 (*see also* language)
community of practice, 29, 42, 47, 53, 64, 94–5, 96, **98–100,** 115, 117 (*see also* interstitial; reproduction)
complete, *see* participation, complete
comprehension, *see* understanding, comprehensive
concept, **38–9,** 48, **121**
    conceptual bridge, **47,** 55, 123
conceptualization, *see* abstraction
concreteness, 38–9 (*see also* dichotomies; formal versus informal; particular; stereotypes)
conflict, *see* access; continuity/displacement; power
continuity/displacement contradiction, 57, 58, **113,** 114, 121

contradiction, *see* commoditization; continuity/displacement contradiction
contrast, *see* dichotomies
contributions, *see* newcomers
control, *see* access; power
conventional theories (of learning), 15–17, 31, 47, 50, 52, 54–5, 56, 57, 65, 94, 95, 105, 121
conversations, *see* language; stories
Cooper, E., 63
copiers, *see* machine repair
correction, 83, 106
Coy, M., 63
craft production, 30, 62–3, 64, 65, 66, 69
critical psychology, 49, 113
critical theory, 51
criticism, *see* correction
culture, *see* historical–cultural theories; meaning, systems of; practice, social
cultural interpretation, 48
curriculum, 41, 71, 84 (*see also* sequence)
    learning, 67, 72, 75, 80, 86, 93, **97,** 100, 123
cycles, *see* reproduction

daily life, *see* everyday life and practice
Davydov, V., 48, 113
decentering, 53–4, 94, 122
decontextualization, *see* sequestration
demonstration, 22, 83, 105
design, 102–3
developmental cycles, *see* reproduction
dichotomies, 33–4, 35–6, 47–8, 50–2, 95, **104–5** (*see also* conventional theories)
didactic structuring, *see* teaching
disconnectedness, *see* sequestration
discourse, *see* language

132

Index

displacement, *see* continuity/displacement contradiction
distributed task, 75
division of labor, 63, 69, 70, 79, 92, 96, 117
domestic production, 69, 70, 117
dreams, 67
Dreier, O., 49
dualism, *see* dichotomies

educational forms, 31, 37, 39, **40**, 65
educational purposes, *see* teaching
educational research, 31
effectiveness (of educational forms), 30, 32, 40, 61, 65, 76–7, 86, 93, 105
Engeström, Y., 48, 49, 63, 114
equipment, *see* artifacts
error, 75, 79, 110
Europe, 63
evaluation, 21, 86, 111–12
everyday concept, 48
everyday life and practice, 18–9, 67, 68, 92, 96, 97, 116
exchange of labor for learning, 64, 76, 78, 115
exchange value, 112
exemplar, *see* mature practice; models
experience, *see* dichotomies

factual, *see* knowledge, acquisition of
Fajans, J., 49, 113
family, 92, 115 (*see also* socialization)
fields, *see* mature practice; participation; transparency
flow, *see* information
formal versus informal, 33, 64, 65, 67, 69–70, 84, 85, 95, 96, 105 (*see also* dichotomies; stereotypes)
Fortes, M., 114
fostering, 70
full participation, 29, **37**, 53, 64, 67, 79, 80, 100, 101, 105, **111**, 114
functionalism, 62

Garner, J., 49
Geer, B., 63
generality, 19–20, 33–4, 37–8, 105 (*see also* abstraction)
generations, 56, 114, 116 (*see also* reproduction)
Giddens, A., 50, 54
glass box, 30, 102
goals, 80, 85, 86, 93, 97, 113, 114 (*see also* mature practice)
Gola, *see* tailors
Goody, E., 63, 69, 70, 114, 115, 117
Greenfield, P., 48
Griffin, P., 48
Grosshans, R. R., 63

Haas, J., 76
habitus, 50
Hall, S., 38
Hanks, W. F., 13
Hass, M., 93
hazing, 76
Hedegaard, M., 48
hegemony, 42
heretics, 116
high school, 99
historical–cultural theory, 23, 31–2, 37–9, 42, 50–1, 61–4, 114, 115, 122
historical perspectives on communities of practice, 58, 99, 101
Holzkamp, K., 49
household, *see* domestic production; family
Hutchins, E., 65, 73, 77, 84, 101

identity, 29, 36, **52–3**, 55, 56, 70, 79, 80, **81**, 84, 109, 112, **115**, 122
of mastery, 41–2, 85, 110–11, 121
illegitimate participation, 35
Ilyenkov, E. V., 38
imitation, 95, 105, 116 (*see also* observation)
improvisation, 15, 20, 93, 97

Index

Index

Index

personal story, *see* stories, personal

perspective, *see* understanding, comprehensive; viewpoints, multiple

phenomenology, 16, 50

physics, 99

place, *see* knowledge

play, *see* work

political economy, 54, 64, 122

power, 36, 42, 57, 64, 86–7, 98 (*see also* access)

practice, social, 29, **34–5,** 43, 49, 58, 95–6, 98, 104 (*see also* community of practice; mature practice; participation; prescription of practice; unintended practices)

   theory of, 14, 16, **34–5,** 38, 47, **50–1,** 52, 121

praise, *see* evaluation

prescription of practice, 64, **96–7,** (*see also* teaching)

prescriptive interpretation (of a concept), 41

production, 47, 51, 56, 67 (*see also* craft; person)

   processes and organization of, 72, 80, 84, 96

   modes of, 63, 70, 114

   structure of, 86

progress, 62

progression, *see* sequence

quartermasters, 65, 66, 67, **73–6,** 84, 86, 91, 96, 99, 101, 102, 111

rationalism, 50, 113 (*see also* conventional theories)

recruitment, 65

reflection, 22, 54, 109, 117

relational perspective, 33, **50–1,** 53, 122

relevance, *see* goal; mature practice; understanding, comprehensive

repetitive tasks, *see* routine

replacement, *see* continuity/displacement

representation, 17–18, 33, 74 (*see also* abstraction; cognitive processes; structure)

reproduction

   of communities of practice, 19, 47, 55–7, 58, 76, 86, **113–17**

   of the social order, 47, 58, 69–70, 113–17, 123

   cycles, 55–7, 70, **98–100,** 121, 122

resources, *see* learning

reward, *see* evaluation; motivation

role, 17, 23

Ross, G., 48

routine, 65, 78 (*see also* particular; dichotomies)

rule, 34, 50

scaffolding interpretation, 48

schooling, 21, 30, **39–41,** 54–5, 61–2, 63, 77, 85–6, 96–7, 99–100, 104, 107, 112, 113, 115 (*see also* teaching; training)

   trade school, 66, 73, 76, 104, 112

schemata, 20

scientific concept, 48

Scribner, S., 107

Sea and Anchor Detail, 74

segments of work, *see* production, processes and organization of

selection, 103 (*see also* evaluation)

sequence, 72, 74, 80, 96 (*see also* curriculum)

sequestration, 21, 40, 100, **104–5,** 109

shift in theoretical perspective, 14, **32–7,** 43

situated activity, theory of, *see* situatedness; learning, situated

situatedness (as a theoretical perspective), 14, 31, **32–4,** 37, 40, 94, 97, 121

skill, *see* knowledge

136

Index

slavery, 70

social, *see* identity; membership; practice; reproduction; structure; transformation; world

socialization, 32, 70 (*see also* children)

sociology, 50

Soviet psychology, 49

specialized occupations, *see* division of labor

specificity, *see* particular

speech, *see* language

spirit mediums, *see* mediums

sponsoring, 91–2 (*see also* legitimacy; newcomers)

Stack, C., 99

Standard Steaming Watch, 74

steel-construction apprentices, 76

stereotypes, 65, 96, 104 (*see also* conventional theories)

stories, 23, 34, 68, 80–4, 106, **108–9**
  personal, **80–4,** 105, 109, 111
  war , 109

structural determination, 54

structuralism, 16–17, 20, 22, 24, 54

structure (*see also* abstraction; curriculum; knowledge; production; sequence)
  activity, 23–4, 51, 67, 75, 97, 112
  cognitive, 15–17, 20, 51
  social, 6–7, 30, 34, 36, 49, 51, 52, 56, 58, 62, 67, 71, 83, 93, 96, 98, 113, 122

student, *see* newcomers; schooling

subject matter, 97, 103 (*see also* mature practice)

supermarket, *see* butchers

tailors, 30, 65, 66, 67, **69–71,** 80, 84, 85, 91, 96, 98, 99, 110, 115

talking about versus talking within, *see* language

tasks, 52, 53, 85, 86, 111 (*see also* curriculum; practice; sequence)

teachers, 29, **56,** 61, 76, 77, 113

teaching, 40–1, 48, 49, 52, 54, 61–2, 76, 77, 86, 94, 96–7, 108, 112, 113–14
  absence of, 68–9, 82–3, 84, 85, **92–4**
  curriculum, 49, **97,** 112, 113–14
  verbal instruction, 22, **105,** 107
    (*see also* language)
  versus learning, *see* learning

technicians, *see* machine repair

technology, 30, 56, 61, 65, 66, **101–3**

tests, *see* evaluation

theory, *see* concept; conventional theories; critical theory; historical–cultural theories; learning, situated; practice, social; relational perspective; shift in theoretical perspective; situatedness

time, scope of, 121

tools, *see* artifacts

trade school, *see* schooling

traditional theories, *see* conventional theories

training, 73, 76, 107
  on-the-job, 77, 104

trajectories of participation, 18–19, 36, 54, 55, 74, 84, 121
  biographies, 56
  careers, 61, 115

transfer, *see* generality; internalization; knowledge, transmission

transformation (*see also* reproduction)
  of the social world, 16, 19, 49, 51, 57, 85, **113–17,** 123
  of persons, 15, 18, 32, 51, **52–4,** 80, 121 (*see also* newcomers, becoming old-timers)

transmission, *see* knowledge

transparency, 20, 30, 56, 75, 100, **102–3,** 105, 123
  fields of, 102

Traweek, S., 100

trivial activities, *see* peripherality

137

Index

Continued from the front of the book

The Learning in Doing series was founded in 1987 by Roy Pea and John Seely Brown